ABLE SEAMAN RNVR

ABLE SEAMAN RNVR

H. J. Messer

MERLIN BOOKS LTD.
Braunton Devon

First published in Great Britain, 1989

For
MY WIFE
a sailor's daughter

ISBN 0 86303 475-6
Printed in England by Maslands Ltd., Tiverton, Devon

To those members of the RND, RNVR, and RNR who served in either or both the First and Second World Wars and who did not return.

The cover design by Edward Taylor is a free interpretation depicting HMS Curlew in one of her many engagements with enemy aircraft.

BIBLIOGRAPHY

The War at Sea by Captain S. W. Roskill DSC, RN
The Campaign in Norway by T. K. Derry
Valiant Quartet by G. G. Connell
Carrier Glorious by John Winton
Nightmare at Scapa Flow by H. J. Weaver
Royal Naval Coastal Forces 1939-1945 by A. J. D. North
HMS King Alfred 1939-1945 by Judy Middleton
Sloops and Brigs by James Henderson
Landing Craft Infantry (Large) by New Jersey Shipbuilding Corporation

ERRATA:

Page 43 First line, last paragraph — fore and aft rig, should read — square rig,
Page vi Lower photograph should read — *Crew of HMML 147*
Page vii Upper photograph should read — POMM, *leading stoker and stoker of HMML 147*

FOREWORD
by Rear Admiral Sir Morgan Morgan-Giles DSO, OBE, GM

The Volunteer has always had an important part to play in our Naval history. During World War II RNVR officers and men, from Ordinary Seamen to Commodore, served world-wide in almost every ship and shore-base — numbering some 48,000 officers and 5,000 men.

Relatively little has been written about the RNVR ratings, so this book fills a gap as well as telling a very interesting story.

The author writes fluently and has a remarkable memory. He has recorded his experiences during the first two years of the war, after which he obtained an RNVR commission: but this book has been deliberately written from a Lower Deck point of view, and 'Lofty' Messer has pulled no punches in expressing the opinions which as a very young rating he then held. Fortunately he had the education to observe his own and his messmates' ideas very vividly at the time — and the fact that the book was written so many years later provides a perspective and a balance which makes it all the more valuable.

I feel that his book has achieved several distinct and useful objectives . . . .

It is extremely interesting as a 'Social Record' of the thinking of a wide cross-section of ratings in those days.

Secondly it provides details about ships and small craft, and wartime living conditions on the messdecks. No Naval officer serving at sea can fail to have felt both amazement and lifelong admiration for the ships' companies who put up with such unspeakable discomforts — yet who still remained efficient and did not lose their endlessly endearing sense of humour.

Also the book gives a vivid account of the experiences and adventures of the author himself, who must have been a brave and enterprising young man. And of course, like all history, it points useful lessons for the future — for example the statement that one incident (quite late on) was 'the first time, at sea, that I ever knew what was happening.' Much of the cynicism which the narrative describes could have been eliminated by better information.

Advances in technology have been formidable in the half-century since the events in this book. Ships, and their weapon-systems, come and go: nowadays 'If it works it's obsolete!' as the Americans say. But through the years one fact remains constant and unaltered. It is that the Sailors — the ships' companies — are the 'greatest single factor.' The author puts this well when he says, about a certain Coastal Forces coxswain . . . . 'He was the best type of Royal Navy Sailor, and there can be no greater compliment than that.'

It is an honour to contribute this Foreword to a book about such men, written by an author who 'knows what he is talking about.'

Morgan Giles.

APPRECIATION

Without the encouragement of my dear friend, John Provost Perkins DSC and Bar, this little work would not have been written. It was his idea that an account of service on the lower deck from the viewpoint of an amateur sailor plunged into a completely alien way of life might be of some interest; not only did he start me off but he pushed, prodded and made absolutely certain that I completed the task. I owe him a great debt of gratitude.

I am grateful also, to Mrs Pauline Hinrich who typed the original manuscript and who, while doing so, was generous enough to allow me to think that there was a modicum of merit in the work.

Finally, it was the appreciation of Mrs Janet Mihell of the Imperial War Museum which gave me sufficient confidence to contemplate publication.

ILLUSTRATIONS

Chapter One

Where my love of the sea came from is a mystery; certainly, it was not inherited from either my father or mother's immediate families for neither could boast of a single sailor, perhaps like Topsy it just grew.

Our annual holiday was spent, every year, at Westgate-on-Sea in Kent. I can remember the excitement as the train pulled into the station, the engine panting with relief and steam escaping from every nook and cranny along the length of each carriage. Then, after we had collected our luggage from the van and seen a porter load it on to a trolley, the guard would wave his flag, blow a long mournful toot on his whistle and with much huffing and puffing which reverberated from the shopping esplanade opposite the station, the train resumed its journey; in straining to be away the engine would shower the town with sparks and soot under the thick cover of smoke which issued from its funnel.

A short taxi ride and we were at our rooms in Adrian Square; there we could smell the sea, the sands, the seaweed and savour all the magic of the seaside. The holiday had begun for the second time; the first was when the cab had arrived at our London home to take us to Victoria Station.

It was during those happy, carefree days that I became fascinated by the sea while being taught to sail, row and generally handle a boat by a fisherman whom we nicknamed Deafy. As my father was deaf as well their conversations were chaotic; Deafy had enormous weather-beaten ears into which father would all but disappear as he endeavoured to make himself understood. The monosyllabic replies and grunts which emerged from a well chewed pipe stem were as irrelevant to subsequent events as the frequent nods of the head and touchings of the salt stained peaked cap with a horny forefinger, for Deafy taught me what he considered necessary and not what a pesky landlubber thought to be important.

Starting from basics I learnt how to anchor and then how to heave up the anchor. This I did many times until I could do both without falling over the side. Then I learnt how to row, to scull and how to bring a boat into the beach, through the surf, stern first.

I learnt how to sail and how to rig a sailing boat, how to come alongside under sail (Deafy's boat had no engine), how to leave an anchorage under sail and, finally, how to 'heave-to'. In between I learnt how to tie knots. Deafy was a hard taskmaster but kind; I grew to love him and I think that he became attached to the rather shy, over-anxious and serious little hero-worshipper that I was as a child.

When I could handle a boat I learnt where fish would be at certain stages of the tide and in differing weather conditions; I learnt to dig for lugworms and how to bait a hook; I learnt that dog fish should be killed before being brought inboard and that they make good bait; I learnt how to handle eels and how to gut and clean fish. Deafy showed me how the depth of water is reflected in the colour at the surface, by the various eddies and the shape of the waves. Above all he taught me to respect the sea, never to take a chance and, always, to double check.

Other holiday highlights were the trips on the Eagle steamers and then, when older I was allowed to make the journey, all alone, from Fresh Wharf, London Bridge to Margate Pier. With me, to this day, are the smells of wet hemp, tar, steam and sea water; there is a vivid memory of the bows rising and falling as they drove through the waves with an eager boy revelling in the sparkling spray which cascaded on to the foredeck and laughing with the wind as it mingled with the spray and swept into his face; the exhilaration of sea, wind and a leaping ship has never left me.

Down below all was mahogany and brass with the builder's name-plate prominent in the embarkation flat. There was the smell of food mixed with nautical smells and, in rough weather the stench of vomit. There were pipes, sea cocks, stairways, saloons, passages and the mass-iveness of iron everywhere.

The engine-room was paradise for a boy; there were the giant pistons, flecked with wet, shiny, yellow grease, nodding their rhythmic dance as they drove the bustling paddle wheels. On the catwalks were stokers clad in grimy white vests and blue trousers, handkerchiefs around their necks, flitting about, wielding large oil cans which they poked into the nooks and crannies of the engines. Steam mingled with the oil and grease to produce a unique smell to be found in all ships.

Prep. school at Margate kept me close to the sea, but seldom on it. However, it was there that I discovered authors such as — Taffrail, Percy F. Westerman, W. W. Jacobs, W. Clark Russell, Joseph Conrad et al. My poetry reading was Kipling, Masefield, Newbolt, Tennyson's 'Revenge' and Matthew Arnold's 'Forsaken Merman'. My heroes were men like

Drake, Grenville, Monck, Hawke, Rodney, Howe and, of course, Nelson! But the characters who influenced me most were the fictitious officers who commanded the destroyers in Percy F. Westerman's books about the Dover Patrol in the First World War. I formed an ambition, fully achieved, to stand on my own bridge and command my own HM ship, while dressed in a bridge coat with a white scarf knotted around my neck.

In 1937 it became obvious that war with Germany was inevitable, so I decided to join the RNVR or RNVSR. Knowing, although but vaguely, a chap on board HMS *President* I telephoned him and received an invitation to the wardroom; my brother and a friend, who both had similar ideas, accompanied me. We were entertained royally and then were whisked off to the doctor. After all the formalities had been attended to we returned to the wardroom for a parting drink and were instructed to return on a prescribed day.

On our return we turned aft into the wardroom where we remet our erstwhile host. Going up to him, full of pride at our new status as naval officers, we offered him a drink; he appeared embarrassed and, blushing, blurted out that we were in the wrong end of the ship, "OK," we said, "we'll buy you one in the other end if that is what regulations require." On arriving at the 'other end' it was explained that we had joined as ordinary signalmen — beings who had never entered our thoughts.

My brother and friend chucked it immediately and walked ashore to join the HAC. When I was left alone on *President*'s messdeck I was approached by a couple of chaps, one of whom offered me a beer, they explained that things were not too bad and suggested that I give it a try. We three became good friends and were separated only when we were called up. I stayed on out of a cussed — though not fully mature — belief that I had no wish to go back on a decision taken. I should and could have joined the RNVSR when I would have gone to sea as an officer at the outbreak of war. However, I had much fun in *President* and made several good friends other than the two already mentioned. Perhaps having an affinity to Don Quixote had some bearing on my decision for all my life I have enjoyed tilting at windmills.

The difference between the wardroom and the messdeck was startling. From the ambience to which one was used and, incidentally, which one took for granted, the messdeck was in stark contrast. It was situated right up in the bows and was triangular in shape with the bar as the base.

I have but vague memories of the furnishings, but the image that I carry is of the public bar of a busy city pub. Taylor Walker's Main Line, an excellent, dark, strong beer, was obtainable at a few pence a pint;

doorstep sandwiches were served at an equally give-away price. The whole atmosphere was seedy to the utmost meaning of the word and one that was to be avoided in other walks of life.

Looking back I cannot understand what made me stick it out. There were, of course, compensations the chief of which were the friendships which I made and playing Rugby and shooting for the division. In the summer there were weekends at Bisley although the ratings' hut was as different from the officers' as were *President*'s wardroom and messdeck.

At first I was a signalman but found that I wasn't much good at reading semaphore and morse, a handicap which I carried throughout the war; as an officer in Coastal Forces I would guess as much of a signal as I read and, fortunately, almost always guessed correctly. On joining, we were subjected to the usual rifle drill and those of us who had been in the OTC at school (most of my friends, incidentally) found this to be a cake walk. Being reasonably good at rifle drill, and to be truthful liking it, I was an obvious candidate for the various guard duties which the RNVR performed. We lined the route for Royal and other processions, provided the guard at ceremonial occasions and, indeed, paraded whenever required to do so. Being six feet two and a half inches in height I acted as right hand marker which gave me a slight personal boost. On one occasion, at the Crystal Palace, my friends and I shared our sandwiches with the late Duke of Kent who sat down with us on the deck to eat them; he was a jolly decent chap.

I cannot remember a Petty Officer who was not pleasant or able at his job. The same cannot be said of the officers, at least those with whom I was in contact. They were for the most part pompous fools aping the RN and, besides, being far from efficient; several of them were appointed to *Curlew* and I didn't change my opinion of them, on the contrary it was more than reinforced.

My friends and I had been given a hint that we should be commissioned on, or shortly after, the outbreak of war so, being young, irresponsible and, perhaps, naïve not to have enquired further into that hint, we attended our drills, asked not too many questions while preparing ourselves for the coming conflict.

Secretly, we were rather proud of our uniforms — especially when we wore them in public. I remember the first time that I wore mine I was in a train at Baker Street when, to my horror an elderly sailor got into the compartment and sat down next to me. Looking at me in a quizzical way he asked, "Been in long mate?" In reply and thoroughly squashed, I blurted out that I was RNVR, pretty obvious anyway, and not a real

14

sailor. My tormentor had a heart for he treated me as a real sailor and when I got out his farewell was "Cheerio Jack."

In uniform we soon found that girls were easy prey and so was the odd pint from a gullible civilian.

The highlight of the year was the annual fortnight at sea. I had joined too late in 1937 for this but 1938 found me in HMS *Nelson* at the time of Munich; with two friends from *President*, I joined her at Portsmouth as an ordinary signalman.

Once on board, the Master-at-Arms took us under his wing and came ashore with us, on our first run, to make sure that we got into no trouble. He lectured us on all the pitfalls to be found in a naval dockyard — VD, too much beer, homos, etc. That jaunty was extremely solicitous for our well-being and packed us off to the Isle of Wight for subsequent runs ashore where, I suppose, he considered the temptations not to be as great as in wicked Pompey. He made sure that we knew where his office was in the ship so that we could go to him if we needed his help. A thoroughly decent and good hearted man.

Nelson was huge and massive, it took several days of intense exploration to have any idea of where and what everything was. We three RNVR signalmen were allocated to different but adjoining messes, introduced to the killick and then left to fend for ourselves.

I was given a billet in which to sling my hammock and was shown how to do so by the killick who was as motherly as the Master-at-Arms. I cannot remember much about life in the mess and have but a vague memory of the local geography except that I slung my hammock alongside the bulkhead.

Before leaving London, a friend had told me that his uncle, Captain Coltart, had command of HMS *Glasgow* (I think it was) and that he would be glad to have a chat with me if I contacted him. On arrival I found that the ship was lying right ahead of *Nelson*. When I had settled down I asked the killick of the mess what would be the best time for me to contact Captain Coltart and suggested that I might go to see him one day after 'hands to tea' had been piped. It was then that I learned that ordinary signalmen cannot go calling on Captains RN without going through the correct procedure, so with the help of the killick, I made out a request for permission to make my courtesy call. The Commander, a most decent chap, fixed a time and date with Coltart and I was free to go. In fact, I took tea in his day cabin with the CO of *Glasgow* who, I think, was as intrigued with me as I was with him. None, however, were more intrigued than the members of my mess whose questions, on my return, revealed their acceptance of a ship's captain as almost a god.

Before sailing we spent several days alongside in the dockyard and, frankly, apart from the novelty of the whole situation it was pretty boring for we three RNVRs. Nobody was really interested in us, the jaunty thought that we were better off in the Isle of Wight rather than getting in everyone's way on board, so we saw little of the day to day life of a battleship in harbour.

One evening I was leaning over the side watching a contingent of Royal Marines drilling in practice for some ceremonial event. With me was an old three badger from the mess. When I remarked on the smartness of the drill my companion suggested that I wait for the matelots who would be practising later, then, he said, I would see smartness. He was right, the sailors had none of the rigidity of the marines and none of the bark, bite and crash; instead, in their gaiters and with their easy roll, they appeared to float over the ground. My goodness, they were smart and I felt proud to be one of them.

The night before we sailed there was a big party on the quarterdeck. Signalmen could volunteer to derig and restow the bunting and my mess mates persuaded me to join them. For the sailors it was a most enjoyable chore for they were at liberty to finish off whatever food and drinks were left; besides which each sailor who helped received a tip (was it 1/-?) from the wardroom for doing so.

I was assisting in the dismantling of the awning when the Admiral, Sir Charles Forbes, noticed my RNVR cap badge and called me aside. We had a short chat and I returned to my work.

That is another instance of the enormous gulf that existed between life in the wardroom and that on the messdecks. 'Upstairs, Downstairs' was pure democracy compared with it.

Soon after we were at sea the killick of the mess detailed me to get rid of the gash, so off I went to the upper deck and found the leeward side in the time honoured method of the wetted forefinger, then I emptied the bucket into the sea. Before I could turn round I was surrounded by three marines and marched off, carrying the empty bucket, to the Officer of the Watch where I was accused of the serious crime of not using the gash chute which, until then, I didn't know existed. The OOW being a sensible chap didn't put me, an RNVR, in the rattle but must have had a private word with the Commander. On arriving back at the mess and telling my tale, the killick, far from apologizing for not having informed me about the chute, castigated me for being an ass and for bringing the reputation of the mess into question. Then he regaled me with the all too dark and dreadful punishments for which I should prepare myself. At 11.00 the next morning I was piped to the OOW who despatched me, under the guard of two marines, to the Commander's office. The marines being dismissed it was explained to me how the gash should be emptied, the cost of maintaining a clean ship's side, as well as other interesting little things useful to an ordinary signalman in keeping out of trouble. When he had finished, the Commander offered me a chair and produced two glasses and a bottle of gin. We talked about the RNVR, my visit to HMS *Glasgow* and how I was enjoying my time in *Nelson*. After a couple of drinks he sent me back to my mess. He was a fine man. The mess were incredulous when I arrived back.

My introduction to religious worship in the Navy occurred during the sojourn in Portsmouth. On Sunday, church was rigged on the quarter-deck and the lower deck cleared. I am not addicted to priests or their activities, but I found the occasion to be most splendid and awe-inspiring; indeed one that I treasure and shall always remember. The pomp and splendour, the Royal Marines band, the fluttering white ensign, *Nelson*'s quarterdeck overshadowed by her enormous guns, the bare-headed sailors and officers all recalled for me the traditions and invincibility of the Royal Navy. Once again, I felt proud to be part — even so insignificantly — of such a great Service.

However, there is always bad to counter good and so it was on that Sunday. With war apparently inevitable we sang 'Onward Christian Soldiers' and 'Fight the Good Fight'. The padre's sermon exhorted us to take the words of the hymns in their literal and not metaphoric (as intended) sense. In my opinion no priest of any denomination can sustain a belief in war. When, eventually, I was called up I went with pride to serve my country and I had no illusions other than that Nazi Germany had to be destroyed before it destroyed the civilized world. I disliked, and am still not fond of most Germans, but killing them in the name of God was not a reason for joining the RNVR.

At sea I was on the signal bridge when on watch; the *Nelson*, being flagship, it was a busy place as hoist followed hoist in rapid succession. The officer with whom I came in direct contact was the Signal Bo'sun, a warrant officer and a dear old chap who was as solicitous for we RNVRs' well-being as all others appeared to be.

I was on watch when we sailed and was kept fully occupied in replacing the flags in their lockers after the hoists were hauled down. I was fascinated by the manoeuvres as we cast off and left harbour; the Fleet then had to take station on *Nelson* and it was fun to think that I had a hand, albeit a very small one, in assembling the ships. The weather was fine as I remember it and Ordinary Signalman Messer was as proud and as happy as could be to be part of and at sea with His Majesty's Home Fleet.

I forget which way round the British Isles we sailed or, even, for how long we were at sea but, eventually, we arrived at Invergordon and not before I had experienced a bit of a scare.

On the day in question although the weather was fine the wind was fresh and in one of the many fleet manoeuvres the halyard on the top starboard yard became tangled up in a 'bunch of bastards'. Another signal was pending and only Ordinary Signalman Messer was idle, so the Signal Bo'sun ordered me up the mast to deal with the recalcitrant halyard. This was in breach of orders for RNVRs were not supposed to be sent aloft; I did not know this nor would it have mattered much if I had for an order is an order, so up I went.

Nelson had a terrible motion at sea due, largely, to the manner in which she was mutilated under the terms of the Treaty of Washington; she rolled slowly and then pitched into the same direction; up would come the bows and then she would roll the other way, the bulk of her followed by the dipping bows which screwed into the foaming sea.

The main mast had a steel ladder attached and this was easy to climb but the topmast was equipped with a rope ladder which was not too pleasant. I reached the level of the yard and was preparing myself to step out on to the footrope when I felt a tap on my heels; looking down I saw a leading signalman below me, he had been sent up when the Signal Bo'sun had realized his error. However, for my relief to pass would necessitate me releasing my very tight grip on the ladder which I had no intention of doing; it was far easier and much the better of the two evils for me to go out on to the yard, which I did, followed by the leading signalman. The block was the outboard one which obliged us to move out to the very end of the yard and here the panorama was a thrilling sight with ships spread out in every direction; their white ensigns and signal flags cracking in the strong breeze. Up aloft the ship's motion was considerably more than that experienced at deck level. At one moment, together with the yard, I appeared to be heading for the sea when the ship rolled to starboard and spearing the sky as she rolled to port; it was exhilarating.

Having recovered from my initial fear I had no inclination to descend, but speed was the essence of the errand so we freed the halyard and down we went. On my arrival on the signal bridge that old bo'sun actually apologized for his mistake.

The fleet was preparing for war so, at Invergordon, we three RNVRs were drafted back to London a couple of days before serving our full fourteen days at sea.

At Glasgow or Edinburgh (I forget which) we could not get out of the train for, accompanied by other drafts, we had been locked into our carriage. That is how the lower deck was treated in peacetime. I remembered that I knew the son of Lord Stamp (I think that was his name) the Chairman of the LMSR so, squeezing through the open window I presented myself at the Station-Master's office and, in no time, the carriages were unlocked.

The following year was uneventful except that I transferred from signals to gunnery and became part of the anti-aircraft training units.

One of the pleasures of belonging to the RNVR was the hospitality received from the TA. Often I was the only sailor present and, consequently, was plied with booze. The London Scottish were the worst culprits, so great was their generosity that I had to limit both my intake and my visits. The HAC were the least pleasant and looked down their noses at ordinary sailors. However, we invariably managed to beat them at Rugby which gave me much pleasure. The other London territorial regiments were almost, repeat almost, as hospitable as the Scottish.

The war duly broke out and I won a long standing bet on which day it would start. Waiting for the actual commencement of hostilities had been of considerable significance to me in the years from 1936 to 1939, for being so sure that there would be a war had caused me to waste time. There were several journalists who saw through Hitler among them were Negley Farson and Quentin Reynolds; I read all that they wrote and, further, read all Farson's other books. Winston Churchill was the man I admired most of all and was at a loss to understand why he was not heeded. By golly, we were lucky to have got away with it; after the years of Labour advocating disarmament and the Conservatives waffling and sitting on the fence, that we escaped Hitler's clutches was a Churchillian miracle. Those who suffered were the servicemen, obliged to fight the well equipped Germans with First World War weapons. Churchill was ignored by those weasel politicians of the late thirties and Great Britain felt the full effects of their neglect.

What was the sense, I thought, to lay the foundations of a career if it was to be turned upside down in a year or so? Besides, there was the strong possibility that I would not survive a war. So, foolishly, I went to work each morning to earn sufficient money for the present to enjoy myself. I had four jobs between leaving school and September 1939 and, oddly, was never out of work. On leaving one position always did I manage to find another.

I cannot remember the exact day on which I was called up but it must have been before September 3rd as I was at home then, in uniform, listening to the solemn tones on the wireless in which our declaration of war was announced and feeling rather impotent when the air raid siren went.

Having transferred from signals to gunnery, not long previously, I was not included in the original drafts to the Valiant Quartet — *Curlew, Coventry, Cairo* and *Calcutta.* Those drafts had formed the London Division RNVRs' contingency plans for war and had been in existence for some time. Indeed, the men were in the ships by the end of August.

On the day when I was required to report to HMS *President* I donned my uniform, kissed my mother goodbye and went with my father to the waiting taxi. As we shook hands Father said, "Remember that you are an Englishman, Herbert, always do your duty — whatever it may entail." Father was a reticent man who spoke his mind on very rare occasions, so I was much moved by his words and his very firm and warm handshake. It must have been difficult for my parents (as, indeed, all parents), for my brother, Peter, had been called up by the HAC several days previously.

Incidentally, the taxi driver was quite adamant that he would not accept the fare and despite my protestations, took not a penny from me.

Once on board *President* I was issued with my 'Bag and 'ammick' and all those accessories which were considered necessary for a sailor's welfare. One thing I did not have was sufficient warm clothing for, on leaving home, I had scoffed at my mother's suggestion that I should take sweaters, scarves and gloves with me; a decision which soon I was to regret; to this day I am amazed that I made it for I was well aware of how cold it can be at sea.

Most of the ship's company had been drafted so those of us on that occasion were few in number. I was the first out and remember pushing through a small crowd of idle civilians who patted me on the back murmuring "Good luck Jack," as I made my way to the bus which was to take us to Victoria station.

Sitting on top of the bus, about midships on the port side and, as yet, alone, I felt as though I was in fancy dress. Here was Herbert Messer, duly promoted to AB (a surprise which greeted all ODs), a civilian of 23 years and in a few days, sitting clothed in the uniform of a sailor in HM's Navy, waiting to go off to war. Although I had worn the uniform on many occasions, until now it had not been my normal dress and I fidgeted inside it. Apart from the dress it was not unlike going to a new school.

We had been paid two weeks in advance at 14/- per week! However, with my own money I was not hard up and money went much further in those days.

I had made enquiries about joining the Fleet Air Arm as a pilot, but was not even given an interview as I would have been over 23 before passing out! A ruling soon to be changed.

At Chatham Barracks we went through the acceptance routine and were allocated to messes. Again, it was not unlike boarding- school at the start of a new term; a new position of authority in the House. However, once in barracks one was subjected to a feeling of unreality, a feeling as though one had come up against a long, dark, high wall which blocked, completely, all sight of what was beyond. Events on board *President*, the drills, ceremonials and the fortnight at sea were all finite with, at their conclusion, a resumption of one's normal civilian routine. Here, there was no turning back; one had been plunged into a strange life of which one knew but little and with a future which was as obscure as a night walk. Like it or not there was no turning back and that future had to be faced, so there was but one thing to do and that was to buckle down and make the best of it.

One ray of hope remained for, although the half promised commissions did not materialize at the outbreak of war, we were led to believe, before leaving *President*, that after having done our six months sea time, we should be among the first to be considered! 'Put not your trust in princes.'

Many of those called up, whether officer or rating, came in their own cars. The parade ground at Chatham was large but much of it was taken over as a parking lot. There were Rolls-Royces, Bentleys, Lagondas, MGs, HRGs, Aston Martins and all other breeds of car, large and small. So great was the congestion that it was felt necessary by the hierarchy to issue an order insisting on the removal of all cars from the barracks.

After having found my mess and having nothing to do I migrated to the canteen on the advice of a new acquaintance. Half-way through a cup of tea in came a petty officer who ordered all those of us in there to muster in the drill shed. I was taken in hand by a diminutive elderly three badger who advised caution. The drill shed at Chatham was about 75 yards long and the PO took up his station at the far end; my mentor held back so that we were among the last to 'get fell in'. The haul comprised two ranks of sailors both of which spanned the full length of the shed.

21

My new friend had positioned us as the last two in the rear rank at the end away from the PO, looking up at me he said, "Let's f——- off, Lofty before that bastard comes up here." With that he darted out through a door which was immediately to his left with me in hot pursuit. Outside I asked, "What now?"

"Back to the canteen," was the reply, "he won't come in there again." Neither did he!

The messes in the barracks were in large blocks which were named after Admirals; Nelson, Drake, Anson, etc. They were similar to those in a ship and were placed athwartships in rows on either side of a long room down the centre of which were the ratings' lockers. The decks were laid with wooden planks which required scrubbing. The washing facilities and heads were situated on either side at the end of each room. The galleys were beneath the messes on the ground floor.

It was at my first meal in the barracks that I realized the request 'pass the butter please', had as much chance of success as a girl with her knickers off saying 'No' to a matelot.

In my mess were several chaps of a similar social position and who, like me, were chafing to be at sea. We volunteered for everything from monitors to 'Q' ships. To volunteer it was necessary to make out an official request and then hand it to the Leading Seaman of the mess to be forwarded to the upper echelons for consideration. That leading seaman was as fine a man as I have known; he had served with Commander Campbell in 'Q' ships during the First World War when he had been often and highly decorated. His simple philosophy was that during a war death is stalking you so to go looking for it is not the most sensible of things to do. Consequently, as fast as we made out our requests so he tore them up. He would tell us how the 'Q' ships operated but nothing would drag out of him his own contribution. On one occasion, only, he did refer to himself in words something like this — "Don't try to be bloody heroes; when he has to Jack will have both hands for himself. I've seen men pulling each other off a ladder to get to the upper deck of a sinking ship."

He epitomized the members of the lower deck for that is how they projected themselves. Not for them any false heroics but, 'when the blast of war blows in their ears, then do they imitate the action of the tiger, stiffening the sinews, summoning up the blood, disguising their fair natures with hard favoured rage.'

During my few days at Chatham several amusing incidents occurred.

Then, the Wrens lived in the barracks, their block being between the main gate and the canteen. One night, an elderly rating left the canteen with a full cargo of beer well stowed in his ample stomach; espying a young and comely Wren on his starboard bow he decided to give chase and board her, but the lighter craft proved swifter and better armed than expected so he was far from achieving his object when apprehended. That incident was directly responsible for the immediate removal of the Wrens to quarters outside the barracks.

One old boy, over 90 years of age, was called up by mistake but he arrived in the uniform of bygone years, straw hat and an immaculately pressed suit of the time. He stayed in the barracks for a few days and I remember seeing him strutting about upright and proud and even posing for photographs.

There was a buzz that a First World War veteran had been stopped at the gate when going ashore for being improperly dressed as he was not wearing his medal ribbons. After a lengthy altercation he was told, "No ribbons — no run ashore." His reply was that when he returned, duly beribboned, he expected the Officer of the Watch and the guard to be turned out for his benefit. It transpired that he held the VC and he insisted on his rights. It was the last time those on the gate insisted upon theirs. I cannot vouch for the veracity of this incident but the story was on every matelot's lips and I believe it to be true.

After a day or two I met an old chum from *President* who told me that he was off *Curlew* which was refitting in the dockyard. He tried to persuade me, rather against my will, to join the ship and fill a vacancy in the crew. The reason for my hesitancy was that I had been drafted to an AMC (was it *Andania*?) and had a feeling that service in a great liner might be fun; besides I had a yen to be away from RNVR officers and on my own among the Royal Navy.

However, a chat with the killick of the mess made up my mind for me; he was no champion of AMCs and described them as 'floating death traps.' I hastened to hand him my request to join *Curlew*. How right he was for the ship to which I had been drafted was lost, soon after, with all hands in the northern approaches.

Up till then my short time in the Navy had been no more than a game and the feeling of unreality and of being in fancy dress which I had experienced while sitting in the bus outside *President* persisted. In barracks there was not much discipline, few pipes, little dirt, no paint to chip, plenty of hot water, decent heads and no guns to clean; above all, there was no sea to permeate every aspect of life — clothing, locker, messdeck et al. One could sleep ashore, at home or elsewhere, in a bed. Barracks were warm and

23

dry where life was not too different from, for example, boarding-school, OTC Camps or other similar 'hardships' to which one had been subjected in civilian life. Of course, decks had to be scrubbed, the mess, heads and bathrooms cleaned but it was all done at a leisurely pace and in decent conditions. In barracks the lower deck was just about tolerable; they were not, however, the place for a longish stay as I was to discover later.

Chapter Two

I cannot exaggerate the shock which I experienced on joining *Curlew*. It was as though I had stepped off the parapet of time and fallen into the kitchens of some dark ages king. I was reminded of the sudden change in life style when visiting Kungal in Sweden where there is an ancient castle which has, in the middle of the great hall, a large, deep pit into which the lord threw his enemies; there was no escape and the prisoner was dependent on the moods of his captor for his every necessity. So those on the lower deck were each in their own individual pit and dependent on the goodwill and moods of their officers. I use the past tense because I believe that conditions have changed much for the better over the last fifty odd years.

Curlew was in the final stages of a major refit and although we ate and slept on board we were obliged to use the shore washing and heads facilities both of which were pretty primitive. I slung my hammock in a flat called the recreation space as there were no available billets on the messdeck. At first, sleeping in a hammock was a trial as one lay in a completely different position from that in a bed and movement was restricted. Pyjamas were not *de rigueur* so one slept in one's pants and vest, a habit soon adopted and which was most necessary in emergencies. Boots were hung from the clews and the remainder of one's clothes joined them or were used as a pillow. Hammocks are slung from hooks in the deck head and hang in rows fore and aft; most men slept feet forward and so close to each other as to be almost touching. When one became used to it a hammock was a cosy, ideal bed at sea for it stayed still as the ship rolled round it. Only intense pitching could cause discomfort.

One's hammock had to be lashed in the manner laid down in the Seamanship Manual; it was a drill carried out by Nelson's sailors at the time when hammocks formed part of the defence of the ship — 'Distribute the bedding equally over the whole length of the hammock to prevent it appearing, when lashed up, more bulky in one part than another. Then pass the lashing, seven turns being taken, the first being a running eye and the remainder marline hitched. Stand with the right arm against the hammock, looking towards the head and pass the end or whole coil of the lashing, over the hammock with the left hand. Care should be taken that the turns are equidistant also, that the first and last turns are clear of the bedding. Twist the clews and tuck them under the lashing towards the centre.' The hammock (Mick) was then heaved into the nettings. In wartime, at least in *Curlew*, this discipline was not enforced but in peacetime any minor deviation from the set drill would land the culprit 'in the rattle.'

My greatest problem, initially, was keeping clean; I had one suit, (soon remedied by Goldbergs who made No.1s for something like a pound. Incidentally, I ended with three suits Nos.1s, 2s and 3s), one pair of boots, a limited supply of underclothes, flannels and collars. Working in the conditions which prevailed in the dockyard was not conducive to cleanliness and soon I was as filthy as my clothes. Whenever I attempted to wash either myself or my clothes there were always queues of sailors on the same errand. The active service ratings knew the ropes from the start and those RNVRs who had been on board for several days had learnt quickly. Another problem was acute tiredness due to the unaccustomed physical labour.

Over the next few weeks things seemed to sort themselves out although my boots and dhobying remained problems. Salt water stains black boots and mine were well and truly stained so much so that my attention was called to them at Sunday Divisions. No amount of polish made the slightest difference, so I was obliged to buy a second pair for Sunday best and shore leave. Later I acquired a pair of shoes for tiddley runs ashore.

My collars, after my efforts at washing and ironing, were a disgrace; they emerged all crumpled and with the white stained blue where the colour had run. My flannels and underclothes were, likewise, a delicate shade of blue. My problems were solved by a stokers' dhobying firm. My collars had to be replaced as they were beyond redemption, the stained flannels could be used on board and the underclothes didn't show. After the stokers had taken over my laundering, my collars and flannels sparkled and from then on I was clean from top to bottom and from inside to out.

Life on the lower deck as I experienced it in a cruiser was abysmal and without extenuating circumstances of any kind. The discomfort and overcrowding were the lot of all sailors in small and medium sized ships, but in *Curlew* we had an extra burden to bear for, with the exception of the Skipper and the Lieutenant N, most of the officers were a poor lot, humourless and inefficient. Some were RNVR from *President* and others, victims of the Geddes axe, recalled for war service, few of them warranted respect or received it. Two of the most unpopular were Lt. Cdr. Ian Robertson RN and Lt. O. G. Cameron RN, the gunnery officer; both were the worst type of arrogant officer whose treatment of the ratings received for them the lower deck soubriquet for unpopular officers.

The Skipper, Captain B. C. B. Brooke was a man I admired; he was firm, taciturn and, single handed, turned the mostly amateur ship's company into a formidable fighting unit. He did not suffer fools gladly nor did he accept excuses; for him there was only one way, the right one. In action he was cool, able and brave and he handled the ship superbly. For some reason, known only to their lordships, he was not decorated for his work while in command. Perhaps, his face didn't fit; perhaps, he was too much of an individualist; perhaps, he was too outspoken or, maybe, his attitude to fools didn't help. Anyway, for what it is worth he had my deepest respect. He died about eight years ago, a Rear Admiral with a KBE.

On the lower deck one of the greatest problems was brain atrophy. I had my Shakespeare with me but it did little to mitigate the mental vacuum of the existence. To question procedure was a sin as all routines and disciplines were carried out in the time honoured manner from which no deviation was permitted. For example, when the watch, or part of the watch, was piped to hoist a boat, every man had to have a hand on the fall and appear to be pulling whether or not his presence was necessary. I fell foul of this when I found myself at the tail of a very slack fall and completely redundant to the task in hand. Obeying my sense of reality I dropped the fall for I felt foolish just standing there holding it while those in front were taking the strain. A barking PO soon confirmed me in the error of my ways and never again did I not appear to be working. That the system, however petty it might have appeared to outsiders, was successful is proven by the Navy's record but it was not designed for sailors who had the same ability as their officers to size up a situation and to act upon it.

The indignity of the existence was a challenge, it would have been so easy to let go and be sucked into the lotus-eating life of swearing, runs ashore and a complete abandonment of any pretence at thinking for oneself.

Before the war I had worked for a time in Canning Town as a trainee estate agent and property manager; there I had seen men sit down to meals dressed only in trousers and undervests, never dreaming that one day I might do the same. Everything on the lower deck was reduced to its lowest common denominator, there was no subtlety of any kind. Privacy was non-existent, ablutions, evacuations, reading, letter writing, sleeping and eating were all conducted in a bedlam of half-naked, singing, dripping (grumbling), swearing and seldom silent messmates. One early problem was in getting used to the various dialects which, in many sailors, had become so mixed that they were all but incomprehensible. Another was Naval routine which until one had fathomed it left one little time for one's own avocations. The gulf between the messdeck and the wardroom was enormous; it was seldom that an officer spoke to a sailor other than to give him an order.

In *Curlew* there was very little if any obvious homosexuality; most of the upper deck ratings being RNVR that aspect of Naval life was not apparent, although there was one case of a PO and a young stoker. Buggery in the Royal Navy does, of course, exist but that existence is greatly exaggerated. It is severely punished in the modern service and was a capital offence in the sailing navy. Indeed, I saw more homosexuality at boarding-school than during my seven years at sea.

Swearing was not new to me, I had heard much of it in Canning Town; it was the one aspect of lower deck life that I found hard to resist and I regret that I became, and still am, an addict.

As there were so many RNVR ratings on board there were opportunities for serious discussion but the absolute drabness and soul destroying meanness of our existence did nothing to promote any real interest. The officers did organize lectures on topical affairs and other subjects but these soon came to an end as the ratings were better informed than their self-imposed mentors. I have mentioned that neither I nor most of the crew had a very high opinion of our officers and one of their greatest faults was their inability to inspire any confidence in themselves. The Skipper and Lieut. N being exceptions. The latter was both able at his job and reasonable in his approach to those ratings with whom he was in contact. A day or two before the ship was sunk my job was changed to work with him, but as we were at action stations for the whole period the opportunity did not occur.

One's home was one's mess which, in turn, was part of a complete mess. Each section of the crew messed separately so seamen, signalmen and stokers all had their own messes as did the various chiefs and petty officers.

A mess consisted of a series of tables athwartships with down the centre the men's lockers. Above each table, secured to the ship's side, was a cupboard which held the mess traps, bread, jam, sugar, tea and tinned milk together with a small colony of cockroaches which gradually disappeared under the constant attacks of the sailors. This system hadn't changed since the old wooden walls; all that was missing to complete the comparison were the guns mounted between each mess. Indeed, a recent visit to *Warrior* brought back many memories.

At the inboard end of each table, shining brightly, were the mess's fanny and kettle. The method of making tea in the Andrew (Navy) is to take the kettle and place in it two or more spoons of tea per head together with a generous helping of tinned milk, in the galley fill the kettle with boiling water and allow the brew to stand until the colour, even with the added milk, is a dark brown and the consistency of a viscosity unknown ashore; the mixture is then poured into cups heaped high with sugar. When used to it a most satisfying drink. Pusser's kye (cocoa) was almost a meal; a slab of the greasy concoction was sliced into individual cups and then mixed with boiling water, on special occasions a good measure of condensed milk was added. The result was a thick, cockle warming drink especially acceptable on a cold night watch.

In *Curlew* we were on canteen messing which meant that the mess caterer (usually the leading seaman) bought the food, over and above the official issues, from the ship's NAAFI canteen and if he spent more than the Admiralty Allowance the extra was a mess expense. When one got used to it, especially the grease, the food was not bad at all, but it should be made clear that to those of us who were brought up on boarding-school grub all other was cordon bleu.

My first Sunday supper was a surprise for it consisted of a large, raw Spanish onion, a hunk of Cheddar cheese, bread and butter and tea. This was a relic of the old days when scurvy was rampant in the fleet. We all complained and that was the last occasion on which that meal was on the menu.

Each day two ratings were detailed as 'cooks of the mess.' Their chores involved scrubbing out the mess area and the tables and benches after breakfast, washing up and generally making the mess ship shape for morning rounds. Additional duties were preparing food and taking it to and fetching it from the galley, doing all the washing up after meals and stand-easy, 'wetting' the tea for the a.m. and p.m. stand-easy and, if it was decided to have a duff or Yorkshire pudding for dinner the cooks made them. My first duff was spread around the whole messdeck so, after morning rounds, I was requested to set to and clean up those areas to which my duff had drifted.

29

One aspect of the lower deck which made life easier to bear was the comradeship, sense of humour and eternal optimism of the regular sailor. Although most of them had no ambition, hardly thought for themselves but relied, to a great extent, upon the L/S, POs and officers to run their lives, their support for each other was quite touching. I remember on one occasion when not wishing to go ashore I stayed on board to write letters, when a young sailor from a neighbouring mess asked, "Not going ashore Lofty?" and he produced a half-crown which he would willingly have given me although it was probably his last one. Tomorrow was always going to be better, their last ship was their best ship, their present one the worst; there was always the possibility of finding a willing 'party' on the next run ashore; the 'pigs' in the wardroom were their permanent and implacable enemies, Chiefs, POs and L/S were tolerated and re-spected if they warranted it; a grudging respect, also, was granted to those officers who deserved it. Their childlike innocence in many situations was quite moving. The opposite side of their character could be equally exasperating; their 'cut off my nose to spite my face' attitude, their foolish disregard for rules and regulations which resulted in penalties far in excess of the misdemeanour, their susceptibility to the extra pint and the soft calls of the shore maidens. However, what can never be denied them are their fighting qualities, their composure in all difficult situations whether in war or peace and their wonderful sense of humour. One thing which RNVR sailors learned from their time on the lower deck was respect for their active service messmates.

The regular sailor had an ambivalent attitude towards us. He could not comprehend how we could be so utterly ignorant as regards the simple things which he had been doing since his boyhood days at Ganges. We couldn't dhoby, swear, or dress ourselves properly; we didn't under-stand naval jargon or routine; ashore we didn't rush for the first 'party' or spend the night pouring back beer; our penchant for country walks, the books we read and the manner in which we utilized our spare time amazed him. Our speech was too similar to that of the officers and whether or not our 'white paper' had been started we were all considered as transient on the lower deck and on our way to the wardroom. The quartermaster would pipe 'hands to dinner CW candidates to lunch.' Our ignorance was recognized to be the one thing which was in our favour when, eventually, we became officers!

On the other hand while we were in square rig we were members of the lower deck and one of them. So once they realized that we were trying to make ourselves into better sailors and that we were prepared to share their problems and to work and fight alongside them they accepted us with an amused tolerance. They didn't take advantage of our ignorance of naval ways but, on the contrary, if we found ourselves in difficulties they leapt to our aid. (I had a close friendship with a leading seaman named Tozer, who was that rarity on the lower deck a CW candidate.)

Even though they couldn't quite understand us they had a sneaking regard for those of our abilities which did not pertain to seafaring. We could write letters, help with personal problems of both a service and domestic nature and introduce them to the world of books, art and music. My leading seaman friend and I would read Shakespeare aloud together and how he enjoyed it. On the whole we all got on very well, each respecting the other, despite our utterly different backgrounds.

Chapter Three

Curlew was built in 1917 as one of the Ceres class; *Ceres*, herself, being the prototype of the C Class Cruisers. The original ships were, besides *Ceres, Cardiff, Coventry, Curacao* and *Curlew*. Slightly modified were *Carlisle* (1918), *Calcutta* (1919), *Cairo* (1918), *Capetown* (1919) and *Colombo* (1918).

The Ceres ships were 4,290 tons and their dimensions were 451½ft x 43½ft x 14½ft. Their original armament was 5 x 6-inch guns, 2 x 3-inch AA guns and 8 x 21-inch torpedo tubes. Main armour was 3-inch belt, plus 1 inch deck. The steam turbines developed 40,000 h.p. and gave a top speed of 29 knots, although I remember the engineers saying that when pressed *Curlew* made over 30 knots.

Between 1935 and 1939 *Coventry, Cairo, Calcutta, Carlisle, Curacao* and *Curlew* were converted to anti-aircraft cruisers and armed with First World War vintage 4-inch HA guns. All, except *Carlisle*, were earmarked to be manned by gun crews from HMS *President* and our training was to this end. Nearly all saw action before Christmas 1939 and by 1943 only *Carlisle* was still afloat. The remainder were sunk after hopeless battles against impossible odds, all victims of tactical blunders resulting from the incompetent political and military planning and judgements of the pre-war years. *Carlisle* survived until 8th September 1943 when she went the way of her sisters, another victim of a hasty, ill-conceived campaign, this time in the Aegean Sea.

The history of these ships is well documented by G. G. Connell in his book *Valiant Quartet*; the broader aspect of their short wartime lives can be found in any naval history of the period, so I don't intend to dwell on *Curlew*'s battles; it is enough to write that never did she flinch but always gave more than a good account of herself; she was respected by the Germans and admired by those ashore who watched her end; she died fighting in the true traditions of the Navy, her gun barrels so worn that the shells which they lobbed into the air were more dangerous to her than to the enemy. Indeed, she was a valiant ship and the first cruiser to be sunk in the Second World War.

To illustrate the crazy, stupid and old-fashioned thinking behind the ordeals which beset these ships I quote a Commander-in-Chief Nore who, when asked why MTBs and MGBs were obliged to fight in a well outnumbered situation replied in similar words to the following — "Sir, it is the privilege of the Royal Navy to fight against overwhelming odds."

As an anti-aircraft cruiser *Curlew* was armed with ten of the aforementioned, ancient 4-inch guns on single HA mountings which could be elevated to 90 degrees; originally there were no gunshields! Forward was mounted an eight-barrel, 2-pounder, pom-pom (the Chicago piano) which made a lot of noise but did not live up its bark. It could only fire forward or on one other bearing at a time so the German aircraft came in astern or on several bearings when making their attacks. At the after end of the superstructure deck was a hand operated .5 mounting which was all but useless. Later on Nos. 6 and 7 4-inch guns were removed as they endangered the ship when on certain bearings, so reducing their field of fire as to make them unnecessary burdens. At the same time gunshields were fitted to the remaining 4-inch replacing the splinter mats which their lordships had considered ample protection from the German dive-bombers.

A mere three ships were fitted with RDF (radar) at the beginning of the war and *Curlew* was the only one of the Quartet to be equipped with it although the others were fitted with it later. As she was one of the few ships in the entire fleet to have the extra eye she operated, on many occasions, as a guardship for the capital ships and aircraft carriers. This, I imagine, accounts for the brief references to her in Roskill's *The War at Sea* (and, indeed, other naval histories) while the movements of the other three are fully documented. Radar was so secret at the beginning of the war that *Curlew*'s movements must have been kept very quiet. Connell's book gives more information for his informants were both official sources and members of the crews. However, in the Norwegian fiords our RDF was not much help for the German airmen were shielded by the high cliffs and could not be detected until they appeared over the top to begin their dive and then it was too late. In the open sea it was a boon, although very primitive, and gave us precious minutes to prepare for the attack.

As an additional warning system *Curlew* had an Air Defence Position which was a platform resembling a bird bath, and that was its nickname, built on the foremast just abaft the bridge. Here were six ratings each sitting on a swivel seat and looking through Admiralty pattern binoculars searching a 60 degrees sector from sea level to an overhead position. There were three reliefs who took over at half-hour intervals. Each watch manned the position for four hours during the regular watches and for two during the dogs. Except to go to the heads or make kye we could not go below during our rest period.

This was my cruising station as opposed to my action station and when the alarm bells rang I hurried to the latter. In bad weather, especially inside the Arctic Circle, it was a most dreary place to be although wonderful for watching the Northern Lights. Rain, snow and hail were handicaps and, often, during gales the spray and, at times, solid water would reach to even the height we were above the deck. Whatever the weather conditions it was vital that we kept a good look-out. One redeeming feature was that being right over the bridge we could hear what was going on.

In true Navy fashion something could always be found to clean so that our rest period was spent either cleaning, sitting on the deck whatever the weather or down below making kye. In good weather during daylight hours I would take my Shakespeare up with me. In bad weather we would wear all the clothes, scarves and pullovers that we could pull on, they were covered by a duffel coat and, over that, our oilskins with, overall, the ubiquitous lifebelt. By now we had been issued with sea boots which, apart from being a great boon, relieved me of my problems with leather boots. 'Comforts', provided seaboot stockings, balaclava helmets, gloves, scarves and sweaters. Even now I wonder if the women who knitted the garments knew how grateful we were for them and how much their efforts did to relieve our discomfort. Nigh on fifty years later I am still grateful.

To add to the extremes of cold and wet the ship's motion, never very steady, was felt far more acutely in the ADP than on deck; all in all keeping a good look-out needed both physical and mental reserves of strength.

To quote Captain Scott — 'Great God, this is an awful place . . . .'

To reach the ADP it was necessary to climb an iron ladder made fast to the mast and then to negotiate a second ladder which was similar to the futtock shrouds of a sailing ship and to enter the platform through a hatch in its deck. At first, with the ship rolling and pitching, this ascent did not appeal but soon it became as routine an event as climbing into a hammock.

The officer in charge of our watch was the aforementioned Signals Officer; he had no sense of humour and did not appear to us to have too much ability and we ragged him mercilessly. On one occasion after a greasy Sunday dinner of roast pork and roast potatoes we sailed, quite unexpectedly, because the *Scharnhorst* and *Gneisenau* were out. It was blowing like hell and as we passed through the boom at Scapa and into the open sea we were met by terrifyingly enormous waves. My watch was on in the ADP and, immediately, we were swept by spray and the spent water from the gigantic waves; our platform performed every evolution and just to sit on the seat was an achievement let alone keeping a good look-out. Tozer and I were off for the first trick and huddled up in what shelter we could find we watched the officer's face as it changed colour from pink, to yellow to green. Maliciously, and in a loud voice, I asked Tozer what his mess had for dinner and, taking my cue, he gave me a graphic account of the richness and greasiness of the roast pork. After my similar reply to his similar question poor Robertson was as sick a sailor as I had seen and, in a solicitous voice I asked him if he would like to be helped below; to his credit he stuck it out until 16.00. In fairness it should be noted that he left the service as Captain Ian Robertson DSO, DSC and bar and had been mentioned in despatches for his work after *Curlew* was hit.

Coming off the first and middle watches the messdeck was a haven of peace. In the dim of the night lights the lines of hammocks swayed rhythmically to the motion of the ship; down there was no wind to penetrate layers of clothing and to strike cold into every bone, no sea to beat against the bows and to fly upwards disintegrating into freezing, soaking, salt laden spray; there was only warmth and the prospect of sleep. Apart from the crack of the bows pounding into a heavy sea, the usual ship's creaks and the hum of the engines, the only noise was the heavy breathing of the sleeping sailors, their every exhalation increasing the all encompassing fug. We stripped off our layers of clothes, hauled ourselves into our hammocks and fell into a deep, dreamless sleep. We slept solidly and unmoving until we were shaken by the watch to be relieved or in the morning when the duty PO 'shook' us in the traditional manner; "Wakey, wakey lash up and stow. The sun's burning your eyeballs out — let go of your cocks and grab your socks. Come on now, out of those hammocks — Wakey, Wakey." As he shouted he walked among the sleeping men poking at some hammocks and punching others. Soon, still half asleep, we were all dressing ourselves and lashing up our hammocks. Different POs had different methods in calling the hands; some stormed in and those not out of their hammocks in double quick time were tipped out on to the deck and into the rattle; others, after the initial 'Wakey-Wakey' would call the men from their 'micks' by more gentle methods which proved just as successful as the bullying. We had a draft of boys on board and the PO in charge of them was, in the best tradition of the service, a pretty tough nut. He carried on with his charges in the same manner as they had been treated at Shotley; any lad who could survive that treatment was an equally tough nut. When he called the hands that PO brooked no delay and ejected many a poor riser from his hammock on to the deck.

When 'shaken' to go on watch we dressed and crept out unwillingly into the cold and uninviting night leaving our hammock in position.

Sleep, due to the lack of it, was as important to us as food, women and privacy. 'All night in' was a bonus when we were allowed it. At sea, even in three watches, seldom did we achieve anything like our eight hours; dawn and dusk action stations, real action stations and false alarms, there was always some reason for us to be dragged from our warm dry hammocks. In harbour when a 'make and mend' (afternoon off — originally to make and mend clothes) was piped, many of us would take the opportunity to sleep; runs ashore, washing, dhobying and other activities just gave way to the need for sleep.

Life at sea, especially in winter and, more especially in the northern waters in which we operated, was a continual struggle against fatigue, cold and damp. On several occasions we spent days at action stations and, moreover, in action for much of the time. During lulls we took it in turns to go below for a spell. I have slept on the messdeck table immediately beneath a 4-inch gun and not heard it firing, so tired was I. In those circumstances hot meals were not possible so we lived on sandwiches, tea and soup as and when they could be provided by the cooks. Ingenious gun crews could, nevertheless, find plenty of excuses for one of their number to be absent either mashing tea or kye. Luck played its part in the lottery for sleep as it was not unusual to be at action stations for hours on end and, at stand down, to find one's the duty watch. If the stand down happened to coincide with the change over and one's was the duty watch, then one was obliged to spend a further four hours on watch and without sleep. Leslie Marrer, who was a stoker, remembers not seeing daylight for three days just before we were sunk. He spent the time on watch, without sleep, down below.

When the action buzzer sounded the prime objective was to get to the gun; the first to arrive took the layer's and trainer's seats and followed the pointers until the actual trainer and layer took over; a shell was fused and loaded into the breech and the gun reported as ready. I was a loading number (one of two) which involved carrying the shells from the deck magazine to the fuse setting machine from where it was loaded into the gun.

At one of the early panics I remember watching in horror, as a marine, in the mad stampede, trod on and so severely damaged our ship's kitten that the poor little thing had to be destroyed. On other occasions ratings, including myself, were caught in the bathroom when action stations sounded and arrived at the gun clad only in a towel; not too pleasant in sub-zero temperatures; as soon as possible, in such circumstances, we were permitted to go below and dress.

In Connell's book there is a picture of *Coventry* covered in ice and snow, it could have been *Curlew*. I have burnt my hand by touching the barrel of a gun in those conditions, ironically, to test whether ice-cold metal does burn. The anti-flash gear which we were obliged to wear in action did help to keep us warm but in hot weather it was stiflingly uncomfortable.

My action station was on ten gun the aftermost one in the ship; it was situated slightly off the centre line to starboard on the quarterdeck. Here the gun's crew were better off than most — especially No. 1 gun on the fo'c'sle — for there was considerable protection from the weather.

Many bombs missed astern and we had a grandstand view of the waterspouts as they exploded in our wake; a less pleasant aspect of these pyrotechnics was the shrapnel zinging around us from these near misses.

At night when star shell and tracer bullets came into their own it was not too fanciful to imagine that I was standing on a seaside pier watching a firework display. Right through the war tracers had a fascination for me; as they arched in a long line across the sky they appeared to hover motionless forming a glittering series of lights, surely too beautiful to be harmful!

The bark of a 4-inch gun is an ear-splitting experience and was complete anathema to me. I hated it and was disturbed by it to such an extent that it is a noise which I shall never forget. After we had been in action for some time the quarterdeck was covered by empty shell cases; these rolled about with the motion of the ship and were a hazard as I ran between the magazine and the gun. It is, however, the memory of the clanging and clatter intermingled with the crack of the gun that makes my ears ring even to this day.

Sometimes, as we sped across the grey, white topped, tumbling North Sea I would watch our heaving wake and, in my mind, travel back along it to England and reflect upon my new existence. These reflections created mixed emotions, for despite all the discomfort and indignities of the lower deck, deep down I was happy when at sea.

37

On joining *Curlew* I was employed 'part of ship' for general work and with the heads cleaning party for special duties. The heads were situated in the forward part of the ship above the messdecks and consisted of about six pans on a dais athwartships, facing aft. Each pan was divided from the next one by a metal bulkhead, raised about eighteen inches from the deck and reaching to sitting shoulder height; a metal door added to the privacy! Needless to say lavatory paper was not too plentiful so newspapers, brown paper, parcelling, cotton waste and, indeed, anything that would do the job was used. Each morning after breakfast, being excused cook of the mess, we performed our domestic task under the eagle eyes of a leading seaman who bore the title of 'Captain of the Heads.' Armed with stiff brooms we swept out the flat as the L/S wielded a hose (again a scourge of my boots); when that chore was finished we hand scrubbed the wooden seats until they were as white as snow and then polished the metalwork until it sparkled. Any failure to achieve perfection resulted in our repeating the entire operation until the L/S was satisfied. The one advantage of this job and it was not to be sneezed at, was that we cleaners were the only ones able to use the heads between breakfast and rounds and, in the evening when we cleaned up before late rounds. Fortunately, soon I was taken off this unpleasant job.

Apart from the damage to my boots I enjoyed scrubbing the decks. Again armed with stiff brooms we marched in line abreast as the Buffer or PO wielded the hose. When it was not too cold as generally it was, this daily routine was carried out in bare feet; the clean, clear gushing water and the motion of the broom had a most pleasing effect on me. Fortunately, in wartime the holystone and the hand scrubber were not utilized.

The hands were divided into three divisions for work and administration; each division being responsible for that part of the ship from which it derived its name; i.e. fo'c'slemen, topmen and quarterdeckmen (mine). The work which consisted of scrubbing, chipping paint, painting, cleaning the brasswork, etc. was done under the watchful eye of the PO of the top who was, in turn, responsible to the Chief Boatswain's Mate (Chief Buffer). Working part of ship was a chore to most sailors for, besides the boredom, it involved being on the upper deck in all weathers. However, before a seaman rating could obtain promotion it was necessary for him to do a stint at part of ship and to satisfy his superiors of his ability in that sphere of seamanship; I would add that unpleasant as the job was it was a vital and necessary part of a ship's efficiency.

The Bo'sun's party were responsible for splicing ropes and wires and all the upper deck seamanship besides which they had charge of the paint and other upper deck stores.

A warship needs more men to fight her than maintain her, consequently it is difficult to find worthwhile employment for all the hands. This results in many not having enough to occupy themselves at full stretch so they resort to skiving and doing as little as possible but, at the same time, trying to give the impression of being hard at work. I found working part of ship to be soul destroying. One incident I remember, most vividly, is when we painted the ship's side in the Humber sometime during November 1939. Ice floes were clanging against the hull and, apart from the cold which was intense, I did not relish being seated on a narrow, swaying, tilting bo'sun's chair which was suspended by lines which I had rove and secured by suspect knots which I had tied. We were supplied with overalls and a good thing too, for soon we were covered in paint.

After a few weeks I was given a new job which I kept until several days before the ship was sunk.

Some of my friends were employed in the gunner's party and, to my surprise, when a vacancy occurred they managed to wangle me in. It was a coveted job as it entailed working below decks and, to a great extent, at one's own speed and as one's own master; but, above all, it meant working in reasonably clean conditions.

Those of us in the gunner's party maintained the magazines under a POGI who was responsible to the commissioned gunner who owed his allegiance to the Gunnery Officer.

Petty Officer Gingell, the POGI, was a short, stocky man, strong as a bull, bouncy, afraid of nothing or anyone, amusing, a born leader and full of that special cunning which always gets the better of authority and which seems to be an integral part of those who had spent some time on the lower deck. A strict disciplinarian, he gave an order once only and, as far as his magazines were concerned, he ruled with a rod of iron. Off duty he was a relaxed and excellent companion who did not and had no need to 'pull rank'; but, never did he come ashore with us and always kept his distance. It did not take us long to appreciate that he accepted and gave friendship but not familiarity.

The magazines contained the 4-inch fixed ammunition — both HA and LA — in boxes containing four shells. The boxes were stacked all round the magazine facing inboard to leave a central space, sufficiently large for the ammunition parties to work efficiently in action when the lid of the box was unshipped and the shells removed after end first.

Each magazine was positioned conveniently for feeding one or more guns. Our job was to stow the boxes and to make them easily available so that the full ones were to the fore. Every so often it was necessary to open a box and examine its contents in order to make sure the shells were in good order and that the contents were shells and not empty shell cases.

The magazines, themselves, had to be kept clean and smart so that, although never stretched, one could always find something to do and if one needed help in the search for work PO Gingell was on hand to assist.

A bonus that went with the job was the gunner's caboose, a small cabin on the starboard side, midships, of the upper deck. Here we would gather to play cards, drink tea or just talk; it was warm and, above all, private. Gingell allowed us to use it after working hours when he was absent, to write letters or simply to read in peace and quiet.

On my first visit to the caboose we played poker and it was an experience that was to serve me well in later years for, despite having very good cards I found myself losing. Puzzled, for I was no novice at the game, it seemed that when I had a good hand nobody stayed in to play and when I was bluffing they were on to me like the proverbial bees round a honeypot. Turning to make myself more comfortable the mystery was revealed; that old fox, Gingell, had put me with my back to his highly polished locker. All the others had suffered the same fate and were without an atom of sympathy so that all I could do was smile rather weakly, cover the locker and try to win back some of their ill-gotten gains. Since then never have I been caught in a similar manner but have to admit to using the ruse on other innocents. In fact, several years later in the Union Club of Trinidad several of us were asked by some locals to teach them how to play the game and, what is more, they insisted on using real money!

Gingell taught me a lesson far more beneficial than never to sit with my back to a mirror when playing cards; he taught me never to say "I can't." The first magazine to which I was assigned was a very small one alongside the boilers and where the temperature was around 45 degrees Centigrade. There was just sufficient space in the centre to remove a box and the boxes, which were pretty heavy, were stowed very tightly. Gingell ordered me to restow the magazine, explained how he wanted it done and then left me to get on with it. Try as I might I couldn't find a way to do it and, after making several half-hearted attempts, gave it up as a bad job. Later, when the PO came down to see how I was getting on I used the fateful words, "I can't see how to do it." He merely reached up, pulled out a box, replaced it and said, "Carry out my order or go back to 'part of ship'." He was half my size and made me feel thoroughly ashamed of myself; after he had gone I thought that if he could do it so could I and I did.

My next and final magazine was in the forward part of the ship; it was quite large and held, besides the 4-inch ammunition, the two-pounder shells for the pom-pom. Having plenty of space in which to work was a great boon and eased the physical side of the job. Like all the magazines this one was below the water line so, at sea, I could hear and feel the pounding as the bows thrust into the waves and the rush of water as it swept past us on each side. Many times did I imagine seeing a torpedo appear through the ship's side or hearing a mine clank against the hull; I had my escape route well planned in case of emergency but, on reflection, would have been lucky if allowed to use it. Down there I learned what it is like for the stokers — sooner them than me.

We had a contingent of Royal Marines on board who, in accordance with Naval tradition manned the penultimate turret in the ship. As we had only single guns theirs was the one forward of 10 gun and situated on the after end of the superstructure deck. Again, traditionally, their mess was between the seamen and officers in order to defend the latter from the former; it was a completely hermaphroditical space, both a barracks and a messdeck. Smells of blanco, gun oil, sweat, brasso and boot polish mingled with the normal shipboard aromas. Like oil and water 'them and us' did not mix although there was no animosity, but simply a distance born of neither side attempting to, or indeed able to, understand the other. I found my explorations into that messdeck to be not unlike visiting a distant part of the British Isles; we were all the same yet vastly different. A Royal Marine is in Kipling's words —

'E's a kind of giddy harumfrodite — soldier an' sailor too.

We had a NAAFI canteen on board which was run by one of the ubiquitous Maltese always found in the job and inevitably named Jose and called Joe for short. There we could buy cigarettes, chocolate (nutty), simple luxury tinned foods and, indeed, anything that Joe thought that it was worth while to stock. It was a most useful place.

I drew my rum ration (tot) which was collected by the cooks of the mess on the pipe 'Up Spirits' and measured out into individual tots by the killick of the mess at dinner; we drank it out of enamel mugs which served as our drinking vessels; it was excellent and helped to dispel some

41

of the misery of the lower deck. I drew but seldom smoked my issue of tobacco (ticklers) for I could not be bothered with all the paraphernalia of rolling my own cigarettes but, more importantly, I preferred Players Navy Cut. Ticklers tobacco, which was very slow burning did have advantages for it was possible, with practice, to roll just the size of cigarette to match the time available to smoke it so, instead of smoking stubs, which were kept in the lining of one's cap, at stand easy and other short breaks a fresh cigarette was possible. These thin, wafer-like fags were called 'stand-easy' ticklers and were the general smoke and hallmark of the mean or hard up matelot. As it was virtually smokeless, a tickler was useful when authority caught one smoking in working hours for it could be hidden, still alight, in a cupped hand and was not so easily detected.

Both rum and tobacco were negotiable and paid for such services as dhobying. Rum was traded or gambled away in quantities from 'sippers' or 'gulpers' to the whole tot. Sailors would stake their tot to support any wild supposition or the latest messdeck buzz (rumour) "My tot says . . . " Needless to say, usually, they were on a loser.

The older hands would soak their tobacco in rum and then roll it up and whip it with spun yarn; the sausage shaped result was sewn up in a canvas jacket and kept in a ditty box until it was mature. When ripe and smoked in a pipe it was quite an experience.

I have mentioned that my mess ate well and often had big eats; a typical day's food might be as follows:

BREAKFAST
When in funds: Bacon, tinned sausages or tinned tomatoes; herrings-in (herrings in tomato sauce).
When short: tea, bread and jam (most often).
DINNER
Straight Rush (Roast meat, spuds, cabbage with a Yorkshire Pudding); Pot Mess (Stew) or Corned Dog (Tinned Meat). These were followed by a duff or tinned fruit when the mess was flush.
Incidentally, *always*, did we eat well at dinner.
TEA
Tea, bread and jam or, perhaps, as supper.
SUPPER
Cheese, herrings-in, sardines or similar things.

Meals would be supplemented by parcels from home which were shared amongst one's messmates.

Tozer, although not in my mess, would let me have some of the marvellous oatcakes which his mother made, and I would return the compliment with something from my parcels.

In harbour, after tea and when not on watch, was when we were able to do all the personal things which are necessary in a sailor's life. At every mess table there were men reading, writing letters, playing uckers (a form of ludo peculiar to the Navy), sewing, dhobying in a bucket, imitating Bing Crosby or the Street Singer (Marta, Rambling Rose of the Wild Wood), preparing tobacco, making models and the inevitable few annoying everybody else.

In other parts of the ship the barber would ply his trade as would the several dhobying firms and the ship's tailor who made jolly smart and well fitting uniforms for almost nothing.

Sometimes, it was pleasant to stay on board when liberty-men were piped for there was an atmosphere of peace on the messdecks during those hours. Now, too, was the time to take a much needed, leisurely, very hot shower and to bask in the feeling of relaxation which hot water provides.

The 16.30 liberty men were given the first use of the bathroom; whether this was a custom throughout the service I don't know, but it was strictly, though unofficially, enforced in *Curlew*; whenever a decent run ashore was in prospect the bathroom was a steaming mass of men shaving, washing and showering (the lucky ones); many making themselves as attractive as possible for the hoped for meeting with a willing 'party' while the older men were solely interested in presenting themselves to the civilians ashore in a reasonably smart and clean manner. Then, all would put on a clean flannel (in summer), a clean collar washed out to a Cambridge blue, No.1s on special occasions but more often No.2s with red badges but, with either, a long ribbon securing the black silk and tied in a neat knot. The tiddley sailor's trousers as wide as regulations would permit, were folded so that the several creases concertina style, were athwartships; the absence of vertical creases was *de rigueur*. In winter an oilskin or greatcoat was donned in a complicated manoeuvre which did not disarrange the collar. On his head, Jack wore his cap with the knot over his left eye. Tiddley aptly described his appearance as he stepped ashore, but maybe not when he returned on board after a particularly rough night.

I have to admit, and am proud to do so, that when in fore and aft rig, my hands in the flaps of my trousers and my cap flat aback, I did not give

43

fourpence for man nor beast. I was AB H. J. Messer of His Majesty's Navy, an unbeatable part of an unbeatable whole. 'Come the three corners of the world in arms and we shall shock them.' Oddly, never did I experience the same absolute raw bellicose feeling when an officer, perhaps the different uniform had a civilizing effect. At no time during the war did I or, indeed, my messmates have any doubts as to its outcome. The Royal Navy with all its tradition just could not be beaten. We knew that deep down in our hearts and believed it implicitly.

On his return on board Jack would let his imagination run riot. "I was in this boozer, see, where I had downed about fourteen pints when in comes this party, cor she was a smasher; she stood in the doorway having a looksee so I strolls over to her and she says 'Mine's a gin and lime.' We have a few drinks and all the time she's giving me the old come on so we strolls over to the park where I says 'Get 'em down love' and down they came. I climbed up her like a rat up a drainpipe, cor she was some screw." In order not to destroy his ego one would intervene with "Really," "No," "Never," "You must have something" and ask pertinent questions about the party. It was a glorious game of make-believe.

Unless the ship was lying alongside a run ashore would, in bad weather, have a miserable start and finish. When the liberty boat came alongside we 'tiddley' sailors climbed into it and were obliged, usually, to stand on the open deck and, if the trip was a longish one we were liable to arrive ashore like drowned rats, all the tiddley shine swept away by salt spray and wind. However, when absolutely chocker (fed up) it was worth the trials to get away from the ship for a short while.

Sometimes when approaching *Curlew* in the liberty boat I would suffer fits of depression. Here was I 'coming home' to this grey warship together with a bunch of drunken messmates. Once on board all the squalor and pettiness of the restrictive life would reinforce themselves after the few hours of freedom ashore. I wondered how much longer I would have to suffer the indignities of the lower deck. To be so utterly reliant on any one else went completely against the grain but to be obliged to be so reliant on officers for whom I had little respect did not help matters.

However, once back into the routine of shipboard life the mood would fade as quickly as it came.

Sailors, being as clean an animal as can be found on this earth, paid particular attention to both their body and their clothes, consequently the bathroom was a popular place. Ours, the seamen's, was quite small, no more than, perhaps, 12ft x 20ft. Along one bulkhead which ran fore and aft were about six basins and opposite, in the after corner, two showers. There was invariably plenty of hot water — except when the condensers packed up — so that the flat which was without ventilation resembled a Turkish bath. Finding an opportunity to shower was no problem in harbour but it was not so easy at sea especially when the Germans interfered without notice. However, all in all keeping clean was not too difficult.

When necessary every largish ship rigged up a mess for those careless enough to catch VD and ours, following tradition, bore the incongruous name of 'Rose Cottage'. Its sole occupants during our nine months' commission were two friends, one married and one single, who came from the same village. The bachelor went on leave first and had a high old time with his oppo's wife, returning with a dose. Then the husband went and he, too, returned infected. It is not difficult to imagine the atmosphere in Rose Cottage when the pair were locked up together.

As already mentioned I wrote letters for some of the sailors whose domestic affairs often were in a hopeless mess and there was little the poor chaps could do about it. Wives were guilty of not writing or, when they did, of giving depressing or rank bad news; some just buzzed off without a by-your-leave, some were having affairs with other men and parents were too often spiteful and foolish in the manner in which they conveyed this news. Most married sailors, of course, had loving and loyal wives but a minority suffered and it was sad listening to their pleas when they dictated what they wished me to write to an erring wife.

There was, of course, the humorous side to letter writing. Before he went on leave Jack would, without blushing, request me to write phrases such as:

Get 'em off and keep 'em off while I'm at home.
Get up them stairs.
Take a good look at the floor for you won't see it again for the next fourteen days.

A ship provides many special jobs such as Bo'sun, Gunner, Blacksmith, Butcher, etc. Each holder of the title had a mate and/or a small party of ratings; it was the ambition of every humble member of the lower deck to belong to and have the security of such a party. Moreover, usually there was a caboose for the use of the members and this provided privacy. There was, obviously, much competition among the sailors to get into a special party for, once in, Jack was almost out of reach of both officers

45

and the ship's normal routine, besides, in the caboose he could have an occasional burn (smoke) and, perhaps, get his head down (sleep) when no one was looking.

Discipline was maintained, under the officers, by the Master-at-Arms (jaunty) and the Regulating Petty Officer (crusher) both of whom, in *Curlew* were decent chaps. I went ashore with the jaunty in Hull but more of that later. Having been on the lower deck softened one's attitude to defaulters when, in time, one was called upon to dispense justice. 'But for the grace of God' was always at the back of one's mind and it can be said, quite positively, that discipline did not suffer.

We had a well equipped sick bay on board; the POSBA, H. Rostron was an extremely nice chap who was most popular with us and we with him. Around the 9th May I was in the sick bay for a few days suffering from a very large and very septic carbuncle just above my navel. So large and so septic was it that both the POSBA and a messmate remember it to this day. I know the date to be correct for on that very day we had a terrible accident on the pom-pom causing one of my friends to be brought in dead. At quarters clean guns, through a series of short circuits and although all was set to safe, the gun fired and blew into very small pieces four of the sponging out party. My friend was killed by a tiny, tiny splinter which ricocheted and hit him as he stood at No.1 gun on the fo'c'sle. The POSBA and I pulled off his clothes but the wound was so small and not bleeding that we had difficulty in finding it; anyway he was certainly dead when we received him and even if we had found the wound earlier we could not have done anything for him. He was so young.

The GI, PO Ruggles, took charge without a second's hesitation and soon had the blood, flesh and bone cleared away. Later 'sails' L/S Leslie Howes made up five canvas coffins and had the unenviable job of sorting out the remains into five identifiable bodies. However, when it was discovered that the fifth casualty was the one in the sick bay poor Howes was obliged to empty the five 'coffins' and re-sort the grisly remains into four.

During my stay in the sick bay I had noticed a photograph of a Windmill dancer named Leah whom I had taken out several times before war broke out, the last being only a few days before my call up. It appeared that the MO was heavily involved with her and was not too pleased that I knew her before he did. However, he was a decent enough chap and did not hold it against me. This little incident illustrates how close some of the RNVR ratings were to the officers and, yet, how far apart. I think that, at times, it was embarrassing for both.

When at sea it was not too clever to dispose of the 'gash' at other than stated times which, normally, were at night. All opened tins had to be pierced through the bottom to facilitate their sinking and so reduce the chance of our leaving a trail for the enemy to follow.

The ship was blacked out at dusk and the Officer on Watch was responsible for seeing that no lights were visible.

There were several kinds of leave:

(1)   From 16.30, 17.30 and 19.00 until a time later in the same evening. On make and mend days leave commen -ced at 14.30.

(2)   All night — from the above times until the following morning in time for 'Hands fall in'.

(3)   Weekend — from 12.30 and the above on Saturday until 'Hands fall in' on Monday morning.

(4)   Friday while — Friday, times as above, until 'Hands fall in' on Monday morning.

(5)   Long Leave — as piped.

Ratings were paid every fortnight my first being a North-Easter (not entitled) as I had received two weeks in advance on board *President*. When his name was called the man marched up to the Paymaster's table and at the order 'Off Cap' he removed his cap with the right hand and presented it to the officer who, reluctantly and reverently, placed upon it two weeks' pay. Was it 28/- for an AB? The money could not be placed in the man's hands for there had not to be any contact between rating and officer. Soon after joining the ship I received an income tax demand from the Inland Revenue; I wrote explaining my present circumstances and heard no more!

One of the favourite lower deck pastimes was dripping (grumbling) and when down in the dumps Jack could be heard to murmur "Roll on my f— twelve." Sailors signed on for twelve years.

A little ditty which helped to relieve frustration when sung with all the pent up emotion of which a matelot is capable was:

This is my story, this is my song
We've been in commission too bloody long.
Roll on the *Rodney*, the *Nelson* and *Hood*
This two funnel bastard is no f—- good.

47

Another version:

This is my story this is my song
We've been in commission too bloody long.
Roll on the *Rodney*, the *Nelson*, *Renown*
This two funnel bastard is getting me down.

Both versions could be sung in a variety of ways, but the two most popular were as the aforementioned means of letting off steam and, also, as a lullaby. The latter was quite moving when employed softly during the night watches.

Sometimes an event at meal times would prompt the following:

"And what will you have?" said the waiter
Pensively picking his nose;
"Two hard boiled eggs, you old bastard
You can't stick your fingers in those."

Some of the pipes and orders that amused us were:

Get fell in the bells went.
The canteen's open . . . . The canteen's closed, mind your fingers, (the canteen had a roller shutter).
Anybody here ride a bicycle? To the answer, "Yes, Chief," the reply would be something like this. "Then ride over and pick up those boxes of tinned milk," I fell for that one immediately on joining *Curlew*.
"Fetch the fog lamp." "Where is it Chief?" "In the fog locker."
"We need a rubber headed mallet for this job." "Where is it?" "Ask the Chief Buffer."
"Them what's keen get fell in previous."
Every new boy to the Navy fell for the golden rivet trick.

One's oppo or winger was one's mate or friend. So preoccupied was many a matelot with sex that a friendly greeting was "Had it in, lately, wings?" When chocker (fed up) a favourite expression was "Shave off."
A gormless messmate was referred to as; "He is as wet as a scrubber." When asked to do something for a messmate instead of answering in the affirmative the reply could be; "I'd swim the stokers' bathroom for you wings."

Nothing could daunt our active service messmates. In the middle of the fiercest action and when a ship we were escorting had been bombed and was sinking, inevitably, someone would chant:

Four little merchantmen
Sailing out to sea
One got hit by a bloody great bomb
And then there were three.

If there was one redeeming feature about the lower deck it was serving with such men.

The ship's routine was as follows; the First Lieutenant had to be informed before those pipes marked with an asterisk could be made:

06.20	Call men under punishment.
06.30	Men under punishment fall in.
06.30	Call the Hands.
07.00	Hands to breakfast and clean.
07.35	Out Pipes.
08.00	Hands Fall In.
09.30	Cooks of Messes Fall In. (In *Curlew* we had morning rounds at 09.30.)
10.00	Hands to quarters clean guns.
10.20*	Stand Easy.
10.30	Out Pipes.
11.00	Up Spirits (cooks of messes collect rum).
11.50	Cooks to the Galley.
12.00*	Hands to Dinner.
13.10*	Out Pipes.
13.15	Hands fall in.
14.20	Stand Easy.
14.30	Out Pipes.
15.45*	Clean up decks.
16.00	Hands to tea)it was possible to do both
16.00	Liberty men to clean)
16.30	Liberty men fall in.
16.55	Fire Party fall in.
17.30	Liberty Men fall in.
18.30	Hands to Supper.
19.00	Liberty Men fall in.
20.25	Clean up mess decks and flats for rounds.
20.45	Men under punishment fall in.
20.50	Rounds.
22.00	Pipe Down.

Chapter 4

In Chatham *Curlew*'s refit was progressing too slowly for all concerned; Captain Brooke and his crew were growing impatient as was C-in-C Nore, Admiral Sir H. Brownrigg, who made several visits to the ship in order to speed up the work.

On one of these visits he was accompanied by Winston Churchill. Lower deck was cleared for the great man to speak to us; we mustered on the quarterdeck and so deep were the emotions which he aroused that I can remember every beat of my heart and exactly where I stood, starboard side aft. He reminded us that many in the crew were RNVR and how, in the First World War, the RND which, composed of reservists, had suffered terrible casualties and privations. "You will not meet the same fate as your fathers," he promised us. Then he spoke something like the following:

> "You are aware of the secret which is housed up there (pointing at the RDF hut) and that on no account are you to talk about it. The Nazis have ways and means of extracting intelligence so, should you be taken prisoner of war, you will give your name, rank and number and no other information. As gentlemen and members of both the RN and RNVR I know that I can rely upon you to keep silent whatever foul cruelties the Nazis may perpetrate upon you."

He went on to give us a pep talk saying that the Navy was the bulwark against which the Nazi hordes would beat in vain and so on in his usual inspiring manner.

After he had finished I, for one, was left feeling as important as Drake or Nelson; if captured the Germans could do their worst but not a word would pass my lips. Fortunately, I wasn't tested.

Throughout my time on the lower deck only two people, besides the Skipper, could silence the messdecks and they were Winston Churchill and Vera Lynn. In my opinion the latter did as much, in her way, as the former to remind us that we were fighting for England and freedom; each was an inspiration. Vera Lynn deserves all she has received and more; a truly remarkable woman.

It was while the ship lay in Chatham dockyard that I changed from Herbert to Bob. My new messmates enquired:

"What's your name Lofty?"

"Herbert."

"Christ almighty, Lofty, that's not half a mouthful. Any other names?"

"Bob."

"OK Lofty."

So Lofty it remained except to my close friends who stuck to Bob the name, eventually, used by everybody including my family.

The reason that Bob came so readily to mind was the wire haired terrier that I'd had since I was about eight years old; he was called Bob and he and I were inseparable. The first sentence in my letters from school invariably began with, 'How is Bob?' I could take him round Piccadilly Circus and he would stay to heel, but with anyone else he was wild. I came home on a night's leave from Chatham, just before joining *Curlew*, to be told that he was dead and that his body was lying in the local, nearby churchyard; the parlourmaid had, that very day, taken him for a walk and let him off the lead; the poor old chap was hit by a bus. I found him wrapped in sacking, took him home and buried him in the garden. He is remembered, yet, with much affection. After the war I went back to the house which was no longer ours, the new owner kindly allowed me into the garden where I was overjoyed to find that the rough wooden cross, which I had erected six or seven years previously, was still in place.

At last, on 26th September, we sailed for Sheerness where I had my first run ashore from a ship out in the stream. I was one of very few in the liberty boat but since being at school at Margate and spending holidays at Westgate I had nourished a wish to see the town from where, for so many years, I had heard guns firing at practice targets. Reading naval history and Pepys had added to the fascination. Needless to say I was disappointed.

The following day we sailed for Portland but not before I had incurred the wrath of the Chief Buffer. I was given a section of the starboard waist to secure for sea but my granny knots and bits and pieces of lashings were far from seamanlike and gave him no pleasure whatsoever. I was obliged to repeat the exercise under the eagle eye of a very amused and patronizing leading seaman.

Soon after we had left the dockyard I was informed that no longer could I sling my hammock in the recreation space. Finding a billet in the messdeck seemed impossible so tightly packed were all the other hammocks so, for two nights at sea, I slept lying on those hammocks remaining in the nettings and jolly uncomfortable it was for the nettings were at the forward end of the messdeck, right up in the bows of the ship. The sea wasn't particularly rough but we were pounding into a westerly and the effect on me was rather like sleeping in a fast moving lift which hit the bottom hard at the extremity of its descent. However, immediately the killick of my mess discovered my predicament he organized a billet for me just forward of the watertight door which comprised the portside entrance to the messdeck. Here my length of sleep depended on which way round the PO went in calling the hands. On a port/starboard route I was the first to be shaken but on the reverse way I was the last. A strange fact is that most POs went from starboard to port to my great satisfaction.

The sea was choppy on the way round to Portland, nothing like that which was to come later but, nevertheless, I had the impression that we were sailing through a hurricane. At first, my cruising station was a gun on the port side, amidships of the superstructure deck and my first watch on it, the middle, was a nightmare. Being woken from a deep sleep and being obliged to dress and go out on to the gun was enough but with each roll to port the sea appeared to be dangerously close and, as there were no guard rails, the fear of falling over the side was not easily dismissed. Instead of gunshields we had an anachronistic shot mat (as did all the guns) which did little to banish the sense of exposure to the enemy's fire should we be engaged in action. The biggest torment of all was the cold; it will be remembered that I had spurned my mother's offer of scarves, sweaters and gloves ("sailors don't wear things like that"). On arrival at Portland I phoned home, without hesitation, to remedy my foolishness. To add to my misery I was drenched by cascades of spray each time the ship pitched into a wave. All through the watch orders came to the gun without respite leaving several unhappy RNVR sailors wondering what in the devil they were doing and why they had volunteered to do it. It was as near hell as I could imagine and I am sure that if, in those early days, I had known the expression I would have been found muttering "Roll on my f—- twelve."

We did a practice shoot which produced a touch of drama for after we had fired one round a member of the gun's crew panicked, lost complete control of himself and ended curled up, wedged into the mounting under the gun. He refused to come out so when we ceased

52

firing along came the Chief GI to find out the trouble; despite repeated orders from officers and senior ratings and pleadings from us lesser mortals he still refused to come out. Eventually, the Chief threatened to fire with the rating where he was; I cannot remember if the threat was carried out, I have a feeling that it might have been, but when he did emerge he was a gibbering, shaking wreck. At the time not many of us had much, if any sympathy for him. He left the ship at Portland.

The practice shoot was the first time most of us had heard a gun fire and, moreover, been a part of the operation so this incident had an effect on our morale. We realized that we had surmounted our first hurdle, albeit a pretty low one, and that when we did go into action and meet higher ones we should be in control of ourselves.

It also had an effect on Captain Brooke for it is possible that it was the cause of him addressing us as he did immediately we had secured to our buoy in Portland Harbour. He said that he was going to turn us into men and, what is more, men able to fight and, if some did not have the stomach for that fight then he had both the power and the will to make them see otherwise. Many of the crew thought him to be insulting and his remarks to be unnecessary. I did not agree in the knowledge that I was hopelessly ignorant, as were most of us, in the ways of war in general and a warship in particular. My goodness me, he made good his words but at the expense of humour and the common touch. *Curlew*, though she became a magnificently efficient, fighting unit, was a dour ship. Perhaps, Captain Brooke's knowledge that he had a duff lot of officers besides a completely raw and mostly amateur crew, selected that approach as the best method to achieve his ends. I was with him all the way for Germans were not and still are not my favourite people. *Curlew*'s fighting record proved him to be right.

We stayed at Portland 'working up' until 1st October when we sailed for Scapa. In between, however, there was another dramatic incident in which, once again, I was very close to what occurred. We were streaming paravanes when I was on the fo'c'sle for about the only time that I can remember; it must have been that all hands were required. I was standing inboard of a snatch block and the wire which was rove through it; on the other side was the young leading seaman who was in charge of our part of the operation. Suddenly, the pin holding the face of the block sheared releasing the wire which whipped out almost chopping the L/S in two and carrying him over the starboard guard rails. We didn't find him and, if we had, I am sure that he would have been dead. War being war, after a short search, we carried on with the exercise; the block having been replaced while the sea boat was in the water.

I was stunned because that L/S was the first man I had seen killed and moreover, the first I had known as a friend to die. He had been most kind and helpful to me and, indeed, to all we 'rookies' (I have the feeling that he was the killick of my mess) besides being a charming and handsome fellow. After all these years I remember him well, standing straight in his oilskins and leather sea boots, his knife hanging from its lanyard at his waist and his cap held on by its blue chin strap. He was the epitome of what I had imagined a sailor to be; he was patient with us in our lack of knowledge and led us quietly and efficiently. His death was a loss to the ship and, perhaps, to the service he served so well.

On our way round to Scapa we had to pass through the area where HMS *Courageous* had been sunk by a U-boat on 17th September; periscopes, submarines and torpedoes were sighted in all directions. I have to confess to a feeling of apprehension in coming into contact with the reality of war for the first time.

As we sailed through the beautiful Western Isles in wonderful weather I remember thinking that if this was war then let it continue for another twenty years. The white flecked, blue sky was mirrored by the white flecked, blue sea. White lighthouses stood prominent against a green background and the whole panorama sparkled in the sun. As we sped northwards little rainbow coloured droplets of water flashed over the guard rails to die on the fo'c'sle.

Later that day we encountered a great gale which, while teaching how capricious is the sea, failed to eradicate the memory of the beauty of those earlier hours.

We arrived at Scapa in the wildest of the wild weather that can be experienced up there. I had the first watch as we came to our buoy at 23.45; when I went below that was the last time my cruising station was to be on the midship gun. During the watch the wind had screamed and howled, the ship behaved as all ships do in a gale but, after even so short a time, I discovered that I had 'sea legs' and felt quite happy in how I had weathered my first gale at sea.

In the morning, I went up on deck as soon as I was awake; the wind had dropped to about force 5, a cloud shrouded sun was attempting to light up the wild Orkney countryside. Overhead hundreds, perhaps thousands, of seagulls squawked, rolled and glided, diving on to scraps of food in the water. The noise was unbelievable and as the birds squawked so the sailors squawked back at them, and hurled abusive cries of 'sheithawk' at the wheeling birds. Now, whenever I hear gulls my mind goes back to that morning in Scapa.

The sheer size of the harbour provided the biggest surprise; acres and acres of cold, grey tumbling water with, here and there, the sinister shape of a warship swinging at her mooring. The fleet was not 'at home' and the comparative emptiness of the huge anchorage emphasized our complete isolation from the civilian world; oddly, I had a feeling of peace and contentment as I gazed around at the wildest scenery I had ever seen. It was at that moment that the full realization of how my life had changed became a reality.

We stayed at Scapa 'working-up' until 15th October but, owing to bad weather, we were not able to carry out all the training that Captain Brooke both wished and had envisaged. For the entire ship's company it was an experience but jolly hard work; we went to action stations at all times of the day and night, we did practice shoots, we exercised damage and fire control, we streamed paravanes, we lowered and hoisted the seaboat, we practised man overboard, we came to buoys, we did anchor and cable work and, in fact, we did everything and more that a warship does when 'working-up'. All the time, of course, the normal routine continued and all were obliged to complete our usual work despite the repeated interruptions.

Runs ashore at Scapa were not too popular for there were only the canteens and a cinema. Later on ENSA parties came up to entertain the sailors and the leisure facilities were improved. However, my friends and I found it to be a marvellous place; we walked for miles in the wild and rugged countryside which, together with the bird and animal life, was a complete revelation to us. We were ragged in that we were jocularly accused of stalking 'Wrens in sheeps' clothing' and it must be admitted that a long absence from women makes a sailor very, very randy; even a week at sea has its effect. There being no women at Scapa, within our reach, we chose exercise as the antidote.

We had a commissioned gunner named Gribbon whom we nicknamed 'King of the Khyber Pass'; his voice was stentorian, his bearing regal and his face reddened by his only fault — his thirst. When the remainder of the ship's company paraded on the morning following the day we had been sunk he was the only one of the survivors, including the Captain, to appear properly dressed. This, despite the possibly apocryphal story that he had been blown under the ship by the explosion. Where he obtained his clean shirt and collar, uniform and cap is a mystery that he has kept to himself. One thing that is certain is that Gieves did not have a branch in Harstad.

The 'King' was in command of the shore patrol on the one occasion when I was a member of it. We had gaiters and belts issued, were inspected and off we went to assist in maintaining discipline among the hundreds of men enjoying their few hours of leisure in the canteens. It was explained to us that the normal practice for patrols was to steer clear of those huts in which gambling games, and especially Crown and Anchor, were being played. It was strictly taboo as the odds were so very much in favour of the bank; notwithstanding the knowledge that they were more likely to lose than to win sailors were drawn to the game as Pooh Bear was to honey. Of course, there was a pay-off for not enforcing the law so that when the patrol paused at the door of the hut beer mysteriously appeared through the aperture. As we marched from hut to hut our paths became increasingly unsteady; the 'King' drinking both whisky and beer was the unsteadiest of all.

Housey-housey was permitted and was played all over the world in every Naval base. There are stories of sailors winning small fortunes on the China Station, sums of money so large that the lucky man would not leave with the ready cash and there are stories of robbery and violence concerning those who did.

On our period of duty being ended we marched, with a very wavering 'King' at our head, back to the jetty which was open to the water on two sides, a small matter which escaped our leader's befuddled brain. Most briskly and, indeed, smartly he marched straight into the drink. Fascinated, we watched him approach his doom but so in awe of him were we and I fear, a trifle mischievous, that not one of us attempted to stop him. He was swearing as only a real sailor can when we fished him out but, though dripping wet, still did he retain his dignity and power of command.

I remember him with affection for, although he was a tough old disciplinarian, he would help even the most humble member of the crew and he was as brave as a lion.

Early on 14th October the action buzzers sounded, it was a pleasant but chilly night and those of us who had been in our hammocks arrived at the gun very sparsely clad. Later, in turn, we went below to finish dressing. Then the rumours started; at first, it was that a U-boat had penetrated the Flow and was cruising around selecting its targets ad lib from the few ships that had returned when the main fleet had gone on to Loch Ewe after completing a sweep. (The defences of Scapa having proved suspect at this early stage of the war.) Then we heard that *Royal Oak* had been sunk. In the meantime we had cast off from our buoy, as did the other ships, and kept on the move while the destroyers hunted for the interloper. We were at action stations for most of the night and much of the next morning. As the starboard ladder was down we, on ten gun, were able to refresh ourselves as the slow speed of the ship allowed us to collect buckets of sea water with which to wash. Around daybreak a requisitioned motor launch, manned by South African VR officers and men came alongside and asked what was going on. We told them what little we knew and, after passing a few pleasantries the CO of the launch, a rather gormless Lieutenant, asked us what he should do! We suggested that he put that question to Captain Brooke and that he warp himself abreast of the bridge to do so. The U-boat was still thought to be in the Flow so we were under way albeit at dead slow ahead and those on the bridge were not free from anxiety. The resulting explosion and chorus of abuse that was heaped on the poor South African Lieutenant's head when he posed his question was, indeed, more akin to the messdecks than the wardroom. Our visitor took the hint and 'f—-off' without delay.

Some time later I met a rating from HMS *Pegasus* which had been lying close to *Royal Oak* and was thus able to pick up some of their survivors; he told me of the horror of their stories and the terrible state in which they were brought aboard *Pegasus*. Apparently, the first torpedo hit either the anchor cable or right forward in *Royal Oak*'s bows for, after the explosion had been both felt and heard no external damage could be found. It was considered that there had been an internal explosion so the hands returned to harbour routine while the damage control parties sought the cause. About an hour later the ship was hit by two more torpedoes; chaos reigned as she capsized and sank within the next thirteen minutes taking with her 883 members of her crew.

Very much later I met a rating who escaped through a porthole. He told me that the messdecks were a mass of flames with men dropping from their burning hammocks into the inferno below; his billet being alongside the scuttle enabled him to get out but not before his hammock caught fire. He was picked up by *Pegasus*.

There was a buzz, unconfirmed, that a torpedo, set to 20ft, had been found on the beach alongside to where we were lying. The Germans claimed the sinking of *Repulse* as well as *Royal Oak*; although much smaller it is possible that at night we could have been mistaken for the battlecruiser. Thank goodness, if the buzz was correct, that we drew a mere 14$\frac{1}{2}$ft.

During the afternoon of the 13th we had gone to action stations when our RDF picked up an approaching plane. Instead of another exercise the stranger turned out to be a Blenheim which flew around and persistently refrained from answering our many challenges. Captain Brooke wished to open fire but the Admiral ashore would not give permission so, after a few minutes, the invader departed.

The suggestion was that the plane had been captured in France, as several Blenheims had been, and was being used by the Germans to photograph the Flow. It is accepted, generally, that Admiral Donitz had planned Prien's attack knowing Scapa's weak defences so photographs of the area would be of enormous assistance to him. Another point to support this theory is that *Royal Oak* was not in the fleet anchorage but was lying in a small bay to the north. Time must have been of the greatest importance to Lt. Prien for he had but two hours in which to carry out his operation; it is more than likely that he had a good idea of *Royal Oak*'s position for it would have been most hazardous for him to have cruised around looking for a target. Whatever the circumstances, Lt. Prien was a very brave man who carried out his mission in an exemplary manner.

From then on, whenever we passed the position, those of us in the ADP could see *Royal Oak*'s silhouette on the bottom of the Flow; it was not a very pleasant sight. In one of those coincidences met so often in life, our First Lieutenant for the second half of the commission was in *Royal Oak* when she sank. He was an Australian, Lt. Cdr. F. Cook, RAN, who later, became his Country's Naval Attaché in Washington.

I am not quite sure when the following incident happened, it might have been March 12. The fleet was moored in two lines, we being at the after end of the starboard column when the base was attacked by German bombers. One chap flew, at masthead with his machine-guns blazing, right down the port column and got away with it. Despite my hatred of Germans I couldn't but respect his courage and audacity; 'even the ranks of Tuscany could scarce forbear to cheer.'

In those early days the Scapa barrage was not up to much and hardly a deterrent to a determined airman. There were a few heavy guns which sounded menacing but, otherwise, were not an effective air defence and there were no short range weapons whatsoever.

On the 16th October we sailed for Loch Ewe to continue our work up. The trip round the north of Scotland was pretty nasty. We, in the ADP, had a fine view of Cape Wrath as we stormed past in the dark buffeted by one of the special gales that blew up there. It was a Wagnerian scene with, on our port side, the steep cliffs throwing back the attacks of the persistent seas which were fragmented by the rugged rocks into harmless white spray. Around us the wind howled as the ship fought her way through tremendous waves, the bows disappearing as they plunged forward, relentlessly, into the solid mass of wild, heaving water which swept across the foredeck, reaching as though to swamp the bridge and, even, us in the ADP high above. *Curlew* was a fine seaboat so, stubbornly, the bows would break free and, rising, thrust the foaming mass from the decks. Every now and then the scene was eerily lit as the moon managed to break through the low scudding clouds. It was a night to remember and I remember it only too well.

In contrast, when we went through bad weather during my sojourns on ten gun, it was as though the bows had broken the sea's will for further onslaughts. The waves which lifted the stern had lost their viciousness and, although flecked with white and spitting spume, they rolled harmlessly into our fast retreating wake. As the stern rose and lifted the screws clear of the sea, they would race and the whole quarterdeck shudder until the ship dropped back into the trough; at first this troubled me but not for long and soon I was used to it.

Loch Ewe is beautiful, a much softer scenery than at Scapa and the anchorage, though excellent, is far smaller than the one we had left. On our first day we caught so many mackerel that we sated ourselves. All that was necessary was the proverbial bent pin or any shiny hook on a piece of string; if twenty hooks were lowered up came twenty mackerel. The cooks in the galleys, both fore and aft, were kept busy in preparing our fish and we did not hesitate in our consumption of them.

On a walk, well inland, my friends and I met an old crofter who, when told that we had never seen an illicit whisky still invited us to inspect his. After a long trek over difficult ground we arrived at an inconspicuous little hut and there before our very eyes was our goal, the illicit still. The product was pretty rough but not sufficiently so for us not to take good advantage of our host's hospitality. When we enquired why he didn't join us he declared that he couldn't drink that rubbish and produced a bottle of Jamiesons!

On the 31st October we sailed from Loch Ewe to escort an incoming Norwegian convoy and the following two weeks operated from Rosyth.

Our next destination was the Humber where we became part of the Humber Force and were employed on convoy patrol. It was here that we painted the ship's side with ice floes beneath our bosun's chairs. God! it was cold that winter.

Around the end of November 1939 came a most unpleasant task; together with *Cairo* and *Calcutta* we patrolled the Thames estuary in a vain attempt to deter enemy aircraft from dropping magnetic mines. Miraculously, we were not blown up as we and the other two ships, were not properly degaussed; we had bits of wire hanging all round us, the ship must have presented a very odd sight. The mines were laid at night by low flying aircraft so our RDF was not much, if any, assistance. I do believe, however, that some good did come out of the exercise for I seem to remember that a magnetic mine was recovered for research.

After ten days of expecting to be blown sky high at any moment, thankfully we sailed for Invergordon all in one piece and stayed there until after Christmas. *Nelson* had been mined and was lying crippled in Loch Ewe so our job was to keep a good look-out, if that is the right expression, with our RDF for enemy planes who might be constrained to attack her. Our stay turned out to be almost a rest cure for the Germans refrained from disturbing us.

My friends and I went to the Union Hotel at Dingwall for high teas after long walks in the beautiful countryside. The proprietress, a very lean, dour, tall Scot, gave us her prior attention much to the chagrin of some of our officers and others who had discovered those excellent teas. In fact there was an attempt to make the hotel out of bounds to the lower deck but our benefactress would have none of it. Either the sailors come or you don't was her declaration and, of course, she won.

Immediately after the war I had to visit Inverness on business and on a nostalgic impulse chose to stay at the Union Hotel. It will be remembered that food was very scarce at that time, even in Scotland, so when the proprietress (the same one) served my high tea on the first day of my stay I reminded her that I used to visit the hotel during the war. "Did ye noo," she replied without showing the slightest interest. Later, remembering how she cosseted us at the expense of the officers, I reminded her that I was a rating at the time. "Were ye noo," she replied again without the slightest emotion but, from then on, I noticed that my plate contained more than those of the other residents.

Christmas Day was not too different from other days except that the messdecks were decorated and the officers served our midday meal. The POSBA provided a tot of 100% proof medicinal alcohol, laced with peppermint, for his more intimate friends of whom I was one. Our rum, following the unexpected drink, made even the messdeck seem attractive. One chap, there is always one, couldn't take it and had to be hidden and kept quiet until he was sober. I had the afternoon watch as a look-out on the port side of the superstructure deck and had the greatest difficulty in keeping awake. Most of the ship's company had shore leave.

We returned to Scapa on 5th January 1940, where we did a few patrols nearly all in heavy seas and jolly wild weather conditions. Then, on 16th January, our luck changed for we sailed south for Hull and leave. I had the first watch on a most unpleasant night when, suddenly, those of us in the ADP became aware of a mild panic on the bridge; the buzz soon reached us with the disconcerting news that we had entered an uncharted minefield. Both Captain Brooke and Lt. Hare remained cool and by proceeding, stern first, on the reciprocal of our original course they saved the ship from probable destruction. After spending the rest of the night in the Firth of Forth disentangling the bunch of bastards into which our paravanes and their towing wires had disintegrated, we continued on our way south.

In Hull eight days leave was piped to each watch — our first of the war — after the ship had entered the dockyard for some much needed work to be done on her.

I was engaged to a girl called Jean whom I had known for several years past and from whom I had taken a passionate and sad farewell on receiving my call-up papers. Our reunion wasn't the romantic event to which I had looked forward but, being half realist and half romantic I wondered, sometimes, if I was expecting too much. Our big night, which I had been savouring all those dreary days and nights at sea, was to be a visit to the Café Anglais where we would dance the night away to Harry Roy's music. Jean asked me to wear evening dress and not my matelot's uniform; rather shamefully I agreed. The club was far from full when we arrived and the emptiness seemed to reflect the spark that was missing between us. At the next table were three Merchant Navy officers, all pretty drunk, who kept making snide remarks about the civilian in 'tails'. For Jean's sake I kept my temper but, eventually, one of them said something particularly personal that got my goat and it was then that I exploded. I offered to fight all three of them at once or separately starting with the loud mouthed one. The offer was accepted so he and I left for a passage which I knew ran at the side of the building. However, before fisticuffs could commence Jean told the other two that I was on leave from the Navy when all three apologized for their behaviour. I was not satisfied and still wanted to have a go at Mr Loud Mouth for I could not forgive his extreme rudeness. By this time Harry Roy, himself, had come to see what the trouble was all about and calmed us all down — especially me. He invited Jean and me to his table and insisted that we be his guests. Besides us the party consisted of Harry Roy's wife, the daughter of the Rajah of Sarawak, her sister and her husband, a wrestler. We drank champagne all night, the band played all my favourite tunes and, as the band was my favourite one I, for one, thoroughly enjoyed myself. I was more than grateful to Harry Roy for his consideration and kindness.

My leave as far as Jean figured in it was not a great success and soon after I was back at sea she wrote to tell me that she had met someone else. Ironically, what galled me most was that he was a civilian. When back, on board, I had realized that my romance was over so was not too cut up at the final parting. Indeed, I indulged myself in the perfidy of women and thought no more of it. The ring came with the letter; its sale provided a few more much needed pints.

The Humber ports, Grimsby and Hull were a sailor's paradise for they were full of brothels, garish pubs and willing 'parties'. They catered for a matelot's ideal run ashore — a f —, a fight and a firkin. The fight was provided by the locals who became pretty hostile after a few pints, and that is not written to relieve Jack of his propensity to enjoy a good scrap but usually, he had to be provoked and then he gave of his best. It is quite fair to say that he did not seek combat but was not averse to it when forced upon him. In Hull the main pub was the Paragon while in Grimsby both the Lincoln Arms and Sheffield Arms (the famous Rat's Nest) had their followers. It was in the latter that I was brought face to face with a life far more basic than anything that I had seen in Canning Town or anywhere else for that matter. A sailor and a girl did a striptease on a bar room table and, when each was stark naked, proceeded to demonstrate the delights of sexual intercourse thus stimulating the appetites of the onlookers. More astonished than shocked for we were no prudes and, indeed, I still am not, my friends and I slipped out as the place erupted. Fisherman fought matelot; beer bottles, ashtrays, glasses and whatever came to hand flew round the bar. Utter bliss existed for the participants until the police arrived and spoiled the fun. Several of Curlew's crew, mostly stokers, came back on board adrift but whether on time or not those who were in that pub arrived with black eyes, smashed noses, sore fists, many in no state to carry out their duties (the yardstick by which drunkenness was measured). The night was talked about, with great tenderness, for many weeks.

On another occasion several of us from the gunner's party went to visit a house where we had been promised a family (?) reception and a quiet, pleasant, satisfying evening. For some reason the jaunty came with us; I believe, because we had told Gingell of our intentions, he had told his sidekick the RPO who, in turn, had informed the jaunty. Apparently, the latter was very suspicious of the area in which the house was situated and, ever mindful of his flock (and perhaps a feeling just a trifle belligerent) he decided to come with us.

When we arrived we were ushered into a ground floor back room which was furnished solely with straightback chairs. There we sat as though in a dentist's waiting-room until a girl came in and announced that 'they' would not be long. Soon the door opened, the jaunty, who was facing it, leapt up crying, "Through the window," and, dashing to the large, bay sash window he smashed it with a chair and was through it, followed by us, rather like a mother duck and her ducklings.

Apparently, when the door opened he saw what he had expected; outside was a band of men all prepared to beat us up and rob us. It was all rather dramatic but a useful addition to our education. Often do I wonder what might have been the result if, but for a lucky chance, that wise old jaunty had not been with us. Indeed, at the time, I was reminded of *Nelson*'s jaunty and his concern for three RNVR signalmen. Masters-at-Arms are devils for discipline but, it would seem, that the welfare of the ship's company is as important to them. Indeed, later in the Paragon our jaunty was buying beer for everyone while accepting all that was offered in return and behaving like a young AB; it was a good run ashore.

I was in the habit of visiting another pub, a rather pleasant one by a river just outside Hull, where the local policeman would come in for a pint after closing time while another frequent visitor was the vicar. On the night in question the vicar arrived in plain clothes and on being asked the reason for not being properly dressed he explained that he had come to the decision that it was not right for him to be dressed as God's agent when in a pub after closing time. An elderly matelot, sitting in a corner, crouched over his beer and sucking his pipe said, very quietly, "But the beer will end up as piss just the same Padre."

Another pub which was popular with Tozer and I was the Crosskeys at Cleethorpes where I became friendly with the landlord's daughter and where, for a few free beers we would help in the bar; on the rare occasions when all night leave was piped it was a good place to stay. I met Jane of the *Daily Mirror* there, she was pally with my girl-friend and was on a tour of the local military camps. The four of us had a jolly evening together.

Our base was Immingham from where there was a tram to Grimsby; we RNVRs used the Ship (now gone like the Paragon at Hull). It was a most pleasant hotel where we could return to a civilized life the memory of which was fast receding and where the landlord and his staff made us most welcome. However, it was used by the Admiral as well as other officers including Mountbatten so it was not long before it was out of bounds to the lower deck. A sad decision for us.

Mountbatten's destroyer flotilla was operating from the Humber and his 'full ahead, full astern' tactics were soon in evidence as he crashed his boat into and badly damaged the wooden piles at Immingham when coming alongside. I met his complete disregard for others again at Dartmouth but more of that later.

The tram terminus at Grimsby was a pretty dreary spot especially on a cold, windy, wet night. On one side was a wooden fence which had taken on a serpentine shape due to the sailors and their 'parties' using it as a prop for their amorous and passionate farewells.

The journey back to Immingham from Grimsby was never very pleasant; usually, 90% of the tram's occupants were as drunk as skunks, many were belligerent and many, of course, were sick. Add to all that the bitter, inclement weather and, when the ship was lying in the stream, the wet and freezing trip out to her, a run ashore could be more a trial than a pleasure. In fact, unless we were lying alongside, I would stay on board and after the 'Ship' was made out of bounds my runs ashore became scarcer and scarcer.

During the refit the two previously mentioned guns were removed, and much needed shields fitted to the remaining 4-inch guns. The ship was fully degaussed as a defence against magnetic mines.

When once more operational, we spent the next month employed in the anti-aircraft protection of East Coast convoys. Apart from the menace from above we had to combat the menace from below but, fortunately, our various anti mine devices worked satisfactorily; although E-boats were about we did not meet them.

Each evening, at dusk, we returned to Immingham and sailed again at daybreak. On our return to harbour a few hours leave was piped but I seldom took advantage of it. In fact, it was only while we were in Hull and lying alongside or in the dockyard that I went ashore with any regularity.

On 22nd March we returned to Scapa and were employed in the anti-aircraft protection of Scandinavian convoys. It was about this time that we were caught in winds of hurricane force and were obliged to shelter in Sullum Voe. In an admittedly limited experience never had I known such conditions; the ship leapt, staggered, lurched, heaved, bucked, rolled and pitched, she was swamped by giant seas until nothing of her could have been visible to an onlooker. Speed was reduced to dead slow but still those enormous waves crashed against the ship as though intent on destroying the interloper which dared to trespass on their

Author in Chatham at outbreak of war.

RNVR parade at Crystal Palace.

HMS Curlew. There is no picture of the ship after her refit in 1939 and the installation of R.D.F.

Some of the crew of Curlew. *Author in the left background.*

School at Harstad where we lived after Curlew *was sunk.*

Group, HMS King Alfred. Davidson, Fuller and author last three, front row. "Paul" Robeson at right of second row.

HMML 147. Author and two of the crew.

At the coaling wharf, Lowestoft.

Lt. D. Wilkie RNVR, and First Lieutenant.

POMM, leading stoker and stoker of HMML 147.

Author and two of the crew of HMML 147.

Author as Sub Lieut. RNVR.

The brig/sloop Wolverine, a typical coastal force vessel of the late eighteenth century.

The author and Dickie Kemp.

A beached torpedoed ship.

HMS Kedah before her refit.

Landing Craft Infantry of US Navy.

HMMTB 187. From a water-colour painting by E. Tuffnell

preserve. Inboard there was chaos, everything that was not secured took advantage of our negligence and revelled in its freedom. It was in the recreation space that the biggest problem developed for the upright piano, stowed there, broke loose from its lashings so those of us off watch in the ADP were called upon to secure it. As the ship pitched and rolled so the piano raced, most violently, from one bulkhead to another mowing down all in its path and crushing the careless. At last, by securing one end of a line and catching that errant instrument in its bight, we managed to tame it but not before several ratings had suffered minor injuries and the piano several dents.

After the warmth and dry of the ship returning to the ADP was not too pleasant; up there keeping a proper look-out was quite impossible for each gigantic wave sent solid water to swamp our binoculars, ourselves and, indeed, everything in its way, so we blessed the comparative peace on entering Sullum Voe. When we sailed a few hours later it was blowing a mere full gale but, by now, that was no abnormality to us.

Some time in early April as *Schamhorst* and *Gneisenau* were making one of their sorties we were operating alone when our RDF picked up an echo from a large surface ship. We went to action stations and, for the first and only time in the whole commission, we heard the order 'all guns load with LA ammunition.' It was pretty rough weather and the confused sea which slapped against the starboard quarter sent clouds of spray over the quarterdeck obscuring the vision of those of us on 10 gun. Long before we saw the target our bridge had been winking out the challenge without any response. Soon, bearing green 15 degrees we saw the silhouette of a large battleship, travelling very fast on the opposite course to ours.

'Prepare to ram, all guns' crews lie down' was the next order as we raced to intercept the huge ship which looked magnificent and menacing as she forged ahead with her turrets trained to starboard, her bow waves white against the dark background. All the time, as we closed, our signal lamp was repeating the challenge still with no reply from the other ship. Lying on the deck I thought that this was rather a tame way to die for should we ram that monster it was obviously us that would suffer the most. But why had those vast turrets not opened fire? The instinct was to be up and firing as we rammed, at least our tiny shells would have some impact on that great hull. But why had she not opened fire? Then, at the last minute a lamp winked across the water, over to port went our wheel and, as we swung away, we recognized *Renown* perhaps just before or after her brief action with *Gneisenau*.

From now on we stayed in Norwegian waters for most of what remained of *Curlew*'s life. I am not going into details regarding her actions for they can be read in Connell's *Valiant Quartet*. However, some observations will help to illustrate the difficulties under which ships and men had to operate in Norwegian waters.

When we covered the landings at Namsos one of the principal transports was a Polish ship, *Chrobry*, which had been loaded with the ammunition and food at the bottom and the inessentials on top. Consequently, when we were obliged to buzz off, those troops who had been landed were left with nothing more than their field rations and a few rounds of ammunition. Not surprisingly, the poor devils were decimated.

We were present at several other landings and evacuations; the worst part was when nothing was happening for it was then that our imaginations began to work overtime as we waited for the next attack by screaming hordes of aircraft. However, once in action all fear would disappear for then there was no time to think of anything but keeping the guns firing.

Back and forward between ten gun and the deck magazine I would hurry carrying shells with no time to think of anything but feeding that hungry breech. When the bastards dived with machine-guns blazing one could but stand and curse them. It is strange how fear embraces one in its frigid arms when the only dangers are thoughts, imagination and one's own frailties.

Norway, of course, had its compensations. The Aurora Borealis, the midnight sun and the beautiful scenery. The latter could be a handicap when the dive bombers slipped over the high cliffs of a fiord to attack without warning. The midnight sun allowed the German aircraft freedom of movement for most of the twenty-four hours and they didn't hesitate to make full use of it. On one occasion we were caught by JU88s in a fiord together with a fellow sufferer, a Fleet Air Arm Swordfish; while we were being bombed he flew around keeping as close to the cliffs as he was able thus denying the Germans a chance to attack. When the enemy planes departed leaving us both undamaged we cheered him on his way as he acknowledged us with a wave.

A wonderful sight was the pack ice in the vicinity of Bear Island where, oddly enough, it did not feel all that cold, perhaps, because the atmosphere was crisp and dry. The sun sparkled on the ice and, for a brief moment, one forgot the war while absorbed in the absolute beauty of nature.

We operated at Namsos, Trondheim and Andalsnes until about 2nd

May when we made a brief return to Scapa but were soon on our way back to Norway sailing, on 4th May, as part of Rear Admiral Vian's squadron which comprised, besides *Curlew, Valiant, Ark Royal, Glorious, Berwick, Coventry* as flagship and ten destroyers. The object of the exercise was to achieve some sort of air parity with the Germans while an airfield was being constructed at Skaanland from which it was hoped to operate both Spitfires and Hurricanes. Incidentally, it was on the way over that we had our mishap with the pom-pom.

One of our jobs, besides acting as an AA guardship, was to pick up the several airmen who crashed when landing on or taking off from the aircraft carriers. We lost one or two pilots and several equally valuable planes.

On 7th May and for the next forty-eight hours we were at action stations repelling continuous and most persistent air attacks as we acted as the AA protection for the other ships in Ofotfiord which were not equipped to defend themselves under these conditions. When the Germans temporarily satiated their appetites we withdrew to Harstad to refuel and re-ammunition ship.

One night when she was returning from England, after repairs to bomb damage, we met *Cairo*; she brought us mail which we read, avidly, at around midnight on the upper deck. I remember talking to a chap I had known in *President* who displayed his duffle coat which had been serrated, like lavatory paper, right down the left side by machine-gun fire; by some miracle he had not been touched.

A buzz started and was soon confirmed that in a few days we were due to sail for Chatham where we would be issued with tropical kit and would then proceed to Gibraltar and the Med. This did not suit me or the others who were hoping to leave the lower deck, for up to the present only two RNVR ratings had left the ship for *King Alfred*; one was the son of a Commodore in the Cunard Line and the other, a particular friend of mine and a townie, had been lucky enough to get the job of Navigator's Yeoman. Once in the Med, we reasoned, we would be completely forgotten but fate, however, interfered with the Admiralty's plans.

A strategic decision had been taken that Bodo must be held at all costs so we returned to Scapa on 14th May. We sailed escorting SS *Chrobry* which had on board a battalion of the Irish Guards, the Guards' Brigade Headquarters and other troops. Besides *Curlew* the escort comprised *Fleetwood, Wolverine* and *Somali*. The Nazis made full use of the midnight sun as they attacked us continually throughout the twenty-four hours. In Vestfiord *Chrobry* was hit and every officer above the rank of Captain was killed; she was sunk, later, by aircraft from the *Ark Royal.* *Somali*, too, was hit and badly damaged so we returned to Scapa escorting her and FS *Foudroyant* arriving on 18th May after a very slow and extremely nerve-racking crossing.

Curlew appeared to us to bear a charmed life for, while all around ships were being hit and sunk the enemy's bombs seemed most reluctant to fall on us; they fell ahead, astern, to port and starboard but not on us; Captain Brooke must take the credit, for his insistence on training had built us into a formidable floating AA battery added to which was his superb handling of the ship. On the bridge, watching the bombs as they dropped, he would give last minute wheel and engine orders and as the stern slewed under the thrust of the screws and rudder we, on ten gun, would see them explode harmlessly in the sea. Once again, I have to express my admiration and respect for the man.

Dryden wrote, 'when fate summons, Monarchs must obey' and so it was with *Curlew*. The *Royal Ulsterman*, carrying troops, stores and ammunition arrived at Scapa, very much behind schedule, on 18th May after an unauthorized stop at Stornoway. In a disgraceful incident quite foreign to normal Merchant Navy wartime behaviour, the majority of her officers and men refused to take her on to Norway; a naval crew was put on board and we (still under orders for the Med) were directed to escort her to Andalsnes where we arrived on 21st May and then proceeded to Harstad to refuel, after which we lay alongside an ammunition ship as AA guard.

We were in a situation which I did not relish and when the Nazis attacked I had considerably less liking for our highly vulnerable exposure to German bombs. However, we survived the raid without too many problems and when it was over we heard voices from the other ship which, during the raid, had every appearance of being deserted but, now every one of its hatches and openings disgorged Chinamen wearing saucepans and similar articles as helmets. Grinning and chattering among themselves they seemed not too worried by the obvious dangers; we passed a few pleasantries with them in sign language and Pidgin English when they disappeared, as if by magic, into the bowels of their own ship.

Some idea of the conditions in Norway may be gathered from the fact that we and the other AA ships were each and I repeat each, using 3,000 shells per week to combat the Nazi planes. Keeping the AA ships supplied was a source of worry for those whose job it was to do so.

We relieved *Coventry* at Skaanland at 02.25 on 23rd May; there we stayed, at action stations, under continuous attack until we were hit at 15.24 on May 26th. We were protecting the building of the airstrip and had achieved the purpose for our presence as, just before the end, a squadron of Hurricanes had flown on to the completed runway.

The continual cradling of shells in my left arm had caused my watch strap to break the skin of the inside of my wrist so I took it off and secured it to the top of the magazine ready to put on again when the immediate attack was over. It was a gold watch which had been a twenty-first birthday present but more of this incident later.

I was taking a shell out of the magazine when the stick of four bombs hit us on the starboard side below the waterline and abreast of where I was standing, blowing the ship's bottom out. The shells bounced out of the magazine clocking me in the face and testicles in particular and everywhere in general; the blast from the explosion and the following wave propelled me over the port guard rails and into the sea. Fortunately, I was still conscious and aware of what I was doing for which, perhaps, the extreme cold was responsible, so I grabbed the guard rails from outboard and hauled myself back on to the quarterdeck. There I came face to face with Lt. Bourgat, the divisional and quarters officer, who had come to my assistance; for the first time I saw the damage which those bombs had caused and said to him, "Look what those bastards have done to our ship."

"You hate Germans, Messer, don't you?" he replied.

Even at this crucial moment I was surprised by this remark for he was a recent addition to the crew and hardly knew me. My reply was a limp, "Yes, I do." On reflection I remembered, much later, an incident which must have been responsible for his observation.

When we were hit, or at least when I had recovered my senses, I lost my temper and, strangely, thought of my prep. school headmaster, dear old Mr Stanley, whom we nicknamed 'Doon'. He had a strange way of urging me to give of my best for he was a shrewd observer of character who had summed me up correctly, even at that early age. "Lose your temper, Herb," he would shout from the touch line when he wanted something special from me in say, a rugger match or whatever. "Lose your temper, Herb," became a catch phrase between us; I won't go as far as to say I was stimulated by the memory of the actual words but I am sure that they were at the back of my mind and had a subconscious effect on me.

'Abandon ship, every man for himself', had been piped but I couldn't allow those Nazis to get away with it for they were still up there on a bearing of green 25 degrees. All our guns were silent, a silence which mortified me so I picked up a shell from those sculling around on the deck, fused it, loaded, trained and layed the gun and fired. This I repeated several times until an order came from the bridge to stop. The shells were just lobbing out of the gun and, due to the barrel being so worn, were more danger to the ship, itself, than the enemy.

Another reason was that Tozer and others, whom I joined were pulling stokers and those ratings trapped below, through the gap where the ship's side had parted from the deck. It would appear that the crack of the gun firing was causing distress to those poor devils, many of whom were scalded or wounded and all covered in fuel oil and badly shocked. The after supply party had fared worst in the explosion but, I suppose, we were lucky to lose only nine dead although quite a few were wounded.

A number of the crew were, by this time, in the sea so Tozer and I climbed to the superstructure deck from where we tossed Carley Floats, rafts and, indeed, anything that would float to them. Then, we and others, attempted to launch the starboard whaler but to no avail.

Lt. Bourgat asked for a volunteer to go below and search the after end of the ship for anyone who might be alive. Remembering the faces of the men whom I had helped to gain the upper deck I said that I would go. Giving me a chance to change my mind Bourgat reminded me that he would be obliged to shut the hatch and fasten the clips after I had gone below, thus effectively entombing me in *Curlew*'s after section.

After arranging a signal to let those, who I hoped would still be there when I had completed my task and was ready to return to the upper deck, know that I was under the hatch, down I went. To the best of my poor memory the lights were not operating and this is corroborated by PO Tel C. H. Estop with whom, recently, I have renewed contact as well as by the fact that I carried a torch which I was obliged to keep clear of the water which, at times, was well above waist level. Estop had a lucky escape as he was below when the ship was hit and reached a hatch just as it was being closed by the damage control party; his shouts alerting them to his predicament.

It is difficult to describe my feelings when the hatch clanged shut over my head obliterating all daylight. I was surprised that I was not as scared as I had feared I would be; strangely, the thoughts that filled my head were that I had been foolish enough to get myself into the situation so had better make the best of it. There could be no going back.

Slowly and methodically I made my way up the port side, passing through or alongside the marines' messdeck, engineers' office, ERAs' mess and, finally, the engineers' workshop. I looked into them all but all were deserted. It was rather eerie to think that I was the only man, alive or dead, in that part of the ship; the atmosphere was redolent of the *Marie Celeste*. Everywhere were traces of what men had been doing before the ship had been hit. Half finished mugs of tea, odd pieces of clothing and other articles were strewn about the messes.

On I went up a narrow passage until I came to a position where I was able to cross to the starboard side. How many watertight doors I went through I cannot recall but I do remember looking back at the first after I had clipped it shut behind me, (as I did them all) and thinking, 'You bloody fool, you're sealing yourself in.'

There was no noise other than my splashing through the dark, cold, oily water. I was interested that the water level was not constant and discovered, later, the reason to be that the ship, out of control, had run on to a reef in the middle of the fiord.

Thigh deep in water in the black confined space of the port passage a panic seized me and, for a brief moment, I was on the verge of retreating but training, both Naval and self-discipline and the awful fear of being branded a coward by others but, more importantly, by myself allowed me to regain control.

The port side was undamaged but when I turned aft I was worried about what I might find, especially in the WT office as one of the sparkers, Fred Butcher, was a friend. However, it was empty but the water covered the table and the morse key; I wondered whether it might be alive with all the electrics around me so I hurried on with a beating heart. In the wardroom flat, that part of the ship which had been most affected by the bombs, the geography was strange and so was the great hole where the deck should have been. Skirting round the ragged edge I saw the body of the Paymaster Commander lying below. Now, for the first time I thought seriously about my position; the honest approach was to go down and make sure that he was dead but I could not see an easy way of climbing up should I need to so do in a hurry. My conscience was salved by the thought that I had heard, earlier, that he was amongst those killed in the explosion. So I was pretty sure that he was not alive. Beyond the body was a tangle of metal in which I knew there were several other bodies; I wondered if there might be anyone alive so I shouted several times but could hear nothing that might be a human voice. I made a half-hearted attempt to climb down in order to cross over and get closer to the damaged area but it seemed pretty obvious that nobody, alive, was down there and, anyway, I was becoming very worried about my own safety. I had no idea for how much time I had been below but it seemed like ages and I wondered for how much longer *Curlew* might float. A quick glance into the wardroom where the furniture was lying helter-skelter in several feet of water; I was tempted to head for the bar and have a swig of whisky but resisted the very strong urge and returned to the hatch to give my prearranged signal. I was relieved to be on the upper deck once again and was quite flattered, when I emerged, at the looks of relief on the faces of those members of ten gun's crew who had stayed by the hatch.

After I had reported to Lt. Bourgat we shook hands and he left the ship by the port side; before going he pressed me to accompany him but I could see that there were still things to do. I returned to the superstructure (boat) deck where Tosh Harding, the cox'n of the skimming dish (Captain's motor boat), was endeavouring to launch his charge; for a while I gave him a hand but the explosion had twisted the boat in her chocks and this, together with the ship's list made the job impossible. Then I went to help the blacksmith and his mate — a fellow RNVR and messmate named Ryan — smash up the RDF equipment; I have a feeling that the Skipper was directing the operation. When that was completed, suddenly I felt so very tired. The effects of my exertions after days without proper sleep were beginning to tell. My tongue was practically in two for I had almost bitten through it, my testicles were swollen and pained me to the extreme while my body was sore from the shells which were forced from the magazine by the explosion; one of them, of course, had to hit the septic hole in my stomach. I was dressed in matelot's trousers and an RNVR Rugby jersey and was covered in fuel oil from the soles of my boots to my chest besides being soaking wet from head to toe and jolly cold.

"I'm going to get my head down," I told Ryan and toddled off to the messdeck; there I unclipped the watertight door and carefully shut it and reclipped it behind me. I made my way through water which was just below the level of my mess table on which I lay down and must have fallen asleep immediately for Ryan had to shake me; fortunately, in the instance, the import of what I had said was clear to him and he had hurried to find me. Following Ryan from the messdeck I insisted on closing and clipping the watertight door. On the port side, at the break of the fo'c'sle, was the motor boat; so low in the water was *Curlew* that ship and boat lay gunnel to gunnel. In the boat was Captain Brooke, his cox'n, the blacksmith and Lt. Hare; quite gently the Skipper said, "Hurry Messer," as I followed Ryan into the boat. I had my back to *Curlew* and didn't see her go as she slipped below the water a few seconds

72

after we had left her, when I turned round there was no trace of her; the time was 17.10 on 26th May, 1940.

I have to admit to a feeling of great pride that I fired *Curlew's* last salvoes at the enemy and that I was the last to leave her. She was, indeed, a valiant ship.

Incidentally, on the same day my brother, Peter, arrived on Dunkirk beaches where he was to spend his 22nd birthday on 28th May.

How our parents — all parents of those serving — must have suffered.

Chapter 5

I cannot remember how Ryan and I were taken to Harstad, I have hazy memories of the interim but they are too shadowy to be of substantive value. The rest of the survivors were ferried across in *Beagle* and billeted in an empty school. Considerable time must have elapsed for when we arrived they were turned in on palliasses which were packed close together in several of the class-rooms. Our messmates, hopefully, had kept a couple of places for us which we reached by stepping over rows of sleeping sailors. Food and drink had been offered but sleep took precedence over both hunger and thirst. My head was throbbing, I was dog-tired and that empty space was as near to heaven as ever I have been. I lay down and fell asleep all in one movement.

In the morning, such is the vitality of youth, I awoke fully refreshed although still feeling the effects of the previous day; my testicles were swollen and most painful, I ached all over, my tongue was very sore causing considerable discomfort when I ate, the hole in my stomach was troublesome and I was covered to chest high by sticky, stinking, fuel oil.

Those of us who were not in hospital or at the bottom of Lavangs Fiord paraded; we were a motley collection but pride in our ship was reflected in the smart drill. The Skipper said the usual things that COs do in those circumstances and announced that the survivors would return to England in the next few days. In the absence of the 1st Lt. I remember the King of the Khyber Pass taking a prominent part in the proceedings.

There was a call for volunteers to remain in Norway in order to man fishing boats which were being used to ferry stores, ammunition and, occasionally, troops up and down the coast. These boats, because of their exhaust noises, were called 'Puffers'. I thought that to stay would be quite an adventure so I volunteered as did a friend from the gunner's party, 'Paul' Roberson and a leading seaman with whom I had been on good terms in the ship. The rest of the ship's company sailed for England, in *Cairo*, on 28th May.

I cannot remember, precisely, where we messed or slept, when ashore, during the remainder of our stay in Harstad but it must have been the school.

After the parade had been dismissed PO Gingell suggested that the gunner's party might visit the wounded. The ward was packed tightly with beds about 18 inches apart, each containing a serviceman. While sitting on the bed of one of our chaps I was talking to a very young soldier who, repeatedly, complained of pain in his feet and pleaded with me to fetch a nurse. When I found one she told me that the boy had lost both his legs and that there was little or nothing she could do for him. Nevertheless, she came with me and soothed her young patient but warned me that on no account should he be told of his loss. Later, the youngster was talking to another visitor, a lad of about his own age who, when asked to do something about the pain, lifted the bedclothes and blurted out, "But you ain't got no legs to 'urt you mate." I can still hear the scream which brought the nurse hurrying back; there were no sedatives or analgesics to spare so I was obliged to assist in holding down the poor chap while trying to talk him back into a state of relative calm. The worry was that his struggles might cause the stumps of his legs to haemorrhage; fortunately, no damage was done other than to his mental condition, when, eventually, I left he was sleeping.

Our wounded were soon on the way home so I did not revisit the hospital.

Paul and I went to different 'Puffers' and as he stayed with his for longer than I with mine we were separated for a short time.

Each 'Puffer' was crewed by a leading seaman and an AB; the reason for our being on board was that the Norwegian skippers could not be trusted on their own. It was not long, however, before the whole exercise was called off owing to the vulnerability of fishing boats to air attack and, more importantly, the small amount of stores and/or men that they could carry.

I made one trip with a most pleasant but very discipline minded killick and a particularly nasty Norwegian. Each leading seaman was issued with a revolver and given very definite orders to use it if necessary. Presumably *Pour encourages les autres.* I remember standing abaft the wheelhouse, pointing the revolver at the Norwegian who appeared to be on the point of jumping ship. The leading seaman was ashore and, before going, he had given me strict instructions to pull the trigger if anything untoward occurred and had threatened me with the direst of the punishments in KR & AI if I failed him. Standing there, watching the Norwegian skipper, I felt rather foolish and wondered whether I could kill or, indeed, hit the man should he decide to run. Added to this was the crowd on the jetty who, at any time, might have taken the skipper's side in the affair. Fortunately, nobody made a move and all ended peacefully. The place had been heavily bombed and was a mess.

Needless to say that when at sea we were both bombed and machine-gunned but the dourness and complete single-mindedness of the leading seaman gave me courage when it was necessary to take the wheel on the occasions the Norwegian dived for cover. That killick acted in the true traditions of the Royal Navy; somehow, he reminded me of C. S. Forester's *Brown on Resolution*.

When the exercise was called off and we were reunited Paul and I were left to kick our heels. There was organization at Harstad for we were paid (I still have the Norwegian notes), we ate and slept but did no real work until the evacuation.

My testicles and stomach were troubling me; I did not wish to become involved with hospitals for once in their grip all is lost and, anyway, compared to those whom I had visited I was OK. Paul had discovered that an army doctor held a daily, open air surgery so, one morning, we joined the long, long queue. When finally my turn came, the doctor, seeing my dress, asked me whether I was a soldier and, on hearing that I wasn't refused to treat me. From then on I bathed my stomach in sea water but, so polluted with fuel oil was the harbour that I have no doubt I did more harm than good. My testicles, by now, were easing off as regards pain but the right one was as hard as a little nut.

The smell of fuel oil nauseates me even to this day; it was all pervading during my search of *Curlew*'s after end, it was all pervading around the water's edge at Harstad and my body and clothes stank of it.

It is interesting that Lt/Cdr. Ian Robertson boasts that he was able to use the C-in-C's bathroom to cleanse himself with, it would seem, no thought for the unfortunate ratings in the same position as himself.

A Royal Marine headquarters ship, *Mashona*, had been beached in the harbour and the buzz was that she was filled with champagne, caviar and other goodies for the officers' mess. The leading seaman from *Curlew* suggested that we should go out to her and bring ashore some of those goodies. We found a whaler and off we went; we boarded the ship by the starboard boarding port and found that she was full of water forward but that the storerooms were not too flooded. We located the champagne together with tins of delicacies which we took up to the boarding port in readiness for loading into the whaler. We were slightly worried that someone in authority might look askance at our enterprise but hoped that a case of champagne would induce him to take a favourable view of it. What we had overlooked was that *Mashona* was a target for the German aircraft and, sod's law being sod's law, they were obliged to attack while we were on board. We were down below when there was a nasty thud from a near miss on the starboard side forward; we ran up to the bridge where we waited, most apprehensively, watching the bombs fall around the stricken ship. When the raid was over we loaded the whaler with our swag and set off for the shore feeling very conspicuous as ours was the only boat moving in the harbour. Strange to say, there were no repercussions and no questions asked. We cannot have been unobserved but, perhaps, it was possible that we had been thought to have been on official business.

A good time was had by us and our friends that night and, indeed, for several more. So easy had been the operation that we had considered having another go but decided against in case we might be trapped aboard the ship should she be hit during a raid. That first bomb was pretty close and we thought our lives to be more important than champagne.

I made friends with a sergeant in the Irish Guards; he was an enormous man whose unit had been decimated and who had found himself on his own. He knew that Harstad was still in our hands but, before he could reach the town, he had to pass through the German lines. Awaiting darkness he stripped off his clothes and lashed them to his pack then, with fixed bayonet and stark naked except for his boots and socks, he charged the enemy yelling blood-curdling Irish war cries. The Nazis were so startled that they dived for cover while Paddy passed through them without a shot being fired. Years later, when in hospital in 1944, I met a Captain Charles Byrne of the Irish Guards; he had been in Norway and knew Paddy so he was able to authenticate the story, not that I had ever doubted it.

The Irishman and I spent as much time as we could in each other's company for the few remaining days of his stay in Norway; he left in the first of the evacuating convoys. Paul and I were separated once again and I cannot remember why. I have a feeling that Paul was crewing the last 'Puffer' which sailed on Royal Naval involvement.

With Paddy I would visit a café which was kept by a young and attractive woman with whom I had become friendly. She served only those whom she liked and as it was the one place in the town, apart from some service messes, where decent food was available it was popular. Paddy and I were always welcome and ate there at least once a day; on one occasion some men from the French Alpine Troops stormed in after having been refused admission; the owner's call for help rallied us to her cause and, in the ensuing fracas, I was hit on the septic hole in my stomach and down I went. On coming to I found my head was cradled in the Norwegian girl's lap while above and astride of us was the massive, majestic frame of Paddy still swinging his rifle by the barrel. Around us, in a neat circle, lay the unconscious bodies of the Frenchmen, felled by the indestructible Irishman. I loved him at that moment.

Soon it became apparent that the evacuation of Harstad was inevitable; Paul and I (united once more) were given the option of joining one of the groups which left on 4th, 5th and 6th June. However, volunteers were needed to embark the soldiers aboard the troop-ships so, once again, we decided to stay. This was a time of organized chaos but, in true British style, the whole great operation went without a hitch and, what is more, completely foxed the enemy as to our intentions.

During the last few days in Norway and, certainly, after the first batch of troops had gone, I wondered if I had been wise in staying. Doubts about whether those of us left would be sacrificed and similar thoughts went through my mind. I had no wish, being Jewish, to be captured by the Nazis and decided, quite definitely, that should the worst happen I would not surrender. Paul and I talked it over and came to the conclusion that we must stick together whatever the outcome. Perhaps, we would reach Sweden or, even, England in a 'Puffer' or some other craft. In the end all our fears were for nothing as we went on board *Royal Manxman* on the morning of 8th June among the last to leave Harstad. Our relief at this turn of events was considerable for as we had loaded soldiers into boats and ferried them out to the troop-ships we had a strong wish to accompany them; besides, there were rumours that the Germans were closing on the town.

The *Royal Manxman* was part of a convoy commanded by Lord Cork who flew his flag in *Southampton*; *Coventry* and several destroyers formed the remainder of the escort. Later on *Ark Royal* and eight more destroyers joined us.

The Germans had planned to attack our ships and shore establishments in Norway in an operation codenamed 'Juno'; for this purpose Admiral Marschall had, under his command, *Scharnhorst, Gneisenau, Hipper* and four destroyers — a formidable squadron. He knew absolutely nothing about our plans for the evacuation of Harstad and sailed from Kiel on the morning of 4th June with the intention of attacking the town on the night of 8th/9th June. Air reports had indicated two groups of our ships and Marschall decided to engage the southernmost one which led

78

to the sinking of a tanker, *Oil Pioneer*, together with her escorting trawler, *Juniper* and, later, an empty troop-ship, *Orama*; the neutrality of a hospital ship, *Atlantis*, was respected. *Hipper* and the destroyers were then detached to Trondheim to fuel while *Scharnhorst* and *Gneisenau* continued the sweep. At 16.00 on 8th June they sighted *Glorious*, *Ardent* and *Acasta* and by 17.40 the aircraft carrier and *Ardent* had been sunk. *Acasta* then steamed straight at her huge adversaries with all guns that she could bear blazing away. At the last moment, before she was overwhelmed and sunk, she managed to fire a salvo of torpedoes one of which hit *Scharnhorst* abreast of her after turret causing much damage. Admiral Marschall decided to call off the operation and his ships returned to harbour. There is no doubt that the brave fight put up by *Ardent* and *Acasta* saved Lord Cork's convoy and the lives of many soldiers and sailors. *Glorious* was caught 'cold' and did not fly off any of her aircraft. Why is a mystery but there are clues, one of which was the foolishness of her Captain in his feud with his Commander (Flying).

Sadly, but not out of character, the Nazis made no effort to pick up the survivors from our ships.

I have learnt, only recently, that if *Curlew* had survived she might have been escorting *Glorious*. *Fabrum esse suae quemque fortunae?* maybe sometimes but, certainly, not always!

The voyage to England was not too pleasant; the ship was packed with troops, meals were served at several sittings although sittings is a misnomer for, having obtained the grub, a difficult enough task in itself, one took it and ate it wherever one could find an unoccupied space. Men were everywhere and even the upperdeck was a dormitory for hordes of soldiers.

Paul and I decided that the officers' quarters were the place for us and there we found a desirable billet in the small passageway off the main port passage which, as is usual in most passenger ships, houses the doors to two cabins. We used this as our sleeping and eating quarters and very cosy it was. In the after cabin was an amiable French Army Lieutenant who, when we engaged him in conversation became quite friendly despite our diabolical French. For some reason he was obliged to vacate his cabin and, before going, suggested that we move in. We were pretty comfortable, now, and took turn and turn about to sleep on the bunk while the other occupied the easy chair. I remember being reluctant, at first, to lie down on the white sheets in my oily, filthy clothes. Obviously, in such circumstances we removed nothing in case we might have to swim for it and I can still feel the sense of shame at the stains which I left

— particularly with my boots. However, they did not deter Paul from lying on them. We took our food to the cabin and, revelling in our privacy, rarely moved from our sanctuary.

Having officers' voices we countered the frequent checks without opening the door but, finally, one sleuth insisted on entering and, although we tried to bluff it out our clothing gave the game away. Very sympathetically and, indeed, apologetically he insisted on our leaving the cabin but, kindly, allowed us to stay until he had found another tenant. We returned to our passage billet when the new occupant arrived; he turned out to be a most unpleasant young Army officer who grumbled at our presence each time he opened the door. We threatened him with physical violence and that quietened him down.

When we sighted tall, green cliffs there was much speculation as to where we were bound. We had steered almost due west for about two days and then had turned due south; whether we docked on the east or west side of the British Isles was anybody's guess; in the end it turned out to be the east and Aberdeen. We disembarked and spent a few hours in the dock area where one of the sights I remember well is of the women gutting herrings; it was their hands, red and sore, which made the deep impression. The warmest memory, of course, is the first sight of dear old Great Britain.

The realization that I was home and safe cannot be transcribed into words. At one period, in Harstad, it appeared that the chances of leaving Norway were not all that great and I would not have bet one halfpenny that the convoy would survive unscathed. Paul and I had walked round *Royal Manxman's* upper deck on many occasions making our plans for an emergency.

We boarded a normal train to the south and mixed with the civilian passengers. Most of us were in makeshift clothing and only a few, whether soldier or sailor, were properly dressed in the King's uniform.

I was still in my matelot's trousers and RNVR Rugby jersey; my clothes and body were caked in stale, dry fuel oil, I was unshaven, filthy and I must have stunk.

We changed trains at Crewe and from there I had a corner seat with my back to the engine, opposite sat a clergyman and his wife and on my left was Paul. The clergyman, in a sanctimonious and condescending voice, asked us from where we had come and, "What dreadful privations have you suffered my sons?" Politely, we answered both his questions but he kept on talking to us ignoring our obvious wish for quiet and, besides, annoying the others in the compartment. After a period of welcomed silence he asked me for my thoughts and, once again as politely as I could I told him that I was more than glad to be home and that I was thinking how beautiful England is. It was mid June and my head was full of Shakespeare, 'This other Eden, demi-paradise,' when I heard from opposite, "You should thank God, my son, for having spared you," and then addressing the compartment as if in church, he continued, "so should all of you, my brothers."

Before I could reply an old stoker, not from *Curlew*, who had previously signalled his distaste for the parson, piped up, "Thank God, be damned, 'e didn't 'elp me or me poor bleedin' mates. I'm alive, cock, because I was on the upper deck chop, chop, 'e didn't 'elp me, mate, I 'elped me bleedin' self."

With that he winked at me and from then on that ass of a cleric kept quiet.

At the London Terminus we were treated royally, it appeared that everyone in the station wanted to shake our hands and/or buy us food and drink. Paul and I even had our photographs taken.

From London we went to Devonport, HMS *Drake*, to be kitted out. We were given the choice of staying in the barracks overnight or going on leave by the night train. We, by now Paul and I had been reunited with the leading seaman, chose the latter. A stay in barracks might have led to anything so we thought it best to get out of the Navy's immediate reach. A quick shave and a shower but still filthy under our new uniforms we bought some tiddey-oggies and some scrumpy and caught the train.

While playing brag with others in the compartment at some time in the night a sailor walked in and asked if he could join us. The newcomer won a considerable sum of money in so short a time that I was most uneasy and suspected him of cheating. After a bit he asked to be excused when he returned to his own seat and promised to come back later. Shortly, there was a rumpus in the corridor and our erstwhile companion tumbled over us pursued by several sailors who had caught him cheating red-handed. The regular matelots extracted a confession from him and then gave him the option of a thrashing or handing over his money. He chose the latter so his not insignificant bankroll was split up between all those who had been cheated; Paul and I took only what we had lost.

My parents had sold our London house which had been bomb damaged and were living with my aunt in a flat at Swiss Cottage. Only my aunt was in when I arrived and she behaved stoically. She assisted me to clean off the fuel oil which was accomplished with the help of several baths and much use of proprietary preparations like Vim. Need-

81

less to say as much effort was expanded, later, in cleaning the bathroom. That I was not and am not too modest is a boon for as I sat in the bath my aunt scrubbed my front and her maid operated on my back but together, they got me clean. My aunt then attended to my stomach which yielded to treatment over the fourteen days of my leave. My tongue was still very sore and my right testicle was as hard as a little nut.

When my mother returned I was a clean, sweet-smelling sailor more than ready to enjoy my leave.

My brother, Peter, had been sent north after his return from Dunkirk so it was several weeks before we met. Indeed, it was several weeks before he was given leave.

One of the high points of a fairly uneventful leave was seeing my abstemious father drunk for the first and only time.

We were attending a family reunion, in Cookham, to celebrate my return when Father overdid it on gin and sherry; he couldn't get out of the taxi and sat, half in and half out, giggling like a schoolgirl.

Before lunch we were sitting in the garden opposite which was an orchard; suddenly a gun was fired to keep off the birds and at the report I was flat on the deck before I realized what I was doing; I felt more than a trifle foolish when I regained my seat.

It was wonderful to be home with my parents and back in dear old England.

L'Aperitif, a restaurant in Jermyn Street figured prominently in my eating habits whenever I could afford to go there and as it happened, it did so twice during this leave; on each occasion I was with a cousin.

Arthur Messer, a couple of years older than me had been like a big brother; our two families lived very close and we children were virtually inseparable from infancy, indeed until the outbreak of war, Arthur rowed for St Paul's School and my brother Peter, Arthur and I could often be seen on the lake in Hyde Park or Regent's Park steaming up and down with Arthur as stroke.

To my delight on my return to England I heard that Arthur was to be married during my survivors leave. On the day in question we lunched together at L'Aperitif — the Captain in the Royal Artillery and the Able Seaman. We had much to talk about besides the war but as Arthur had not left England he was most interested in my adventures during the previous nine months.

Suddenly, we realized that we had no time at all in which to get to King's Cross station and catch the train to Potters Bar where the wedding was being held. Fortunately, there was a taxi outside the restaurant and with the offer of ten bob to the driver if he got us to the station in time we set off on a hair raising drive. Rushing into the station we saw the train wheezing and puffing away from the closed ticket barrier which we hurdled in fine style and closed on the retreating train. A passenger opened a door and we were on board. It was a jolly good wedding.

The other occasion was with my cousin, now Jean Butt, who has always been like a sister to me. She had no brothers and I no sisters. Again our two families were very close.

Jean was in the Mechanized Transport Corps so once again the officer in khaki and the Naval rating appeared at L'Aperitif but this time, as was usual during the war, we were obliged to queue at the entrance. Ahead of us was a four ringed Captain RN and his wife. Luigi, the head waiter, appeared to tell the Captain that there was no table available, then, turning to me he exclaimed, "Ah! Mon Capitaine, mon ami, it is good to see you again, come in, I have a nice big lobster waiting for you."

When I dared to look back I saw the real Captain stalking away in high dudgeon.

Chapter 6

After my leave I returned to Chatham barracks. *Curlew* was a Guz (Devonport) ship and that is why all the survivors were obliged to proceed to HMS *Drake* despite the fact that the London Division RNVR ratings were borne on the books of HMS *Pembroke*; Chatham, therefore, was my home base.

Incidentally, before leaving Plymouth I had to see the famous Aggie Westons, a sailor's rest founded by the woman of that name. It would appear from the affectionate way West Country sailors referred to it that its fame was well merited and would have made old Aggie feel proud.

I was much more of a sailor on my return than I was during my first brief sojourn in Chatham; far more able to take care of myself and far wiser in the ways of the Navy. The first objective was to distance myself from *Curlew* for all her RNVR survivors were due to be drafted to HMS *Naiad*, again under the command of Captain Brooke. As much as I admired and respected my old Skipper I had no desire to be mixed up, once more, with the officers from *Curlew* as I felt that I would spend far longer on the lower deck if I did so. How right I was for many of my erstwhile friends had to wait until *Naiad* was sunk before arriving at KA long after Paul and I had completed our courses.

HMS *Kelly* was being repaired after her encounter with an E-boat; a notice in the Drill Shed announced that all volunteers to join her would be given priority over any other draft so I thought that this would be an admirable way to avoid any possibility of being railroaded into *Naiad*. In the event it was discovered that too many had volunteered so it was a case of last in and first out; I was one of those excluded.

Paul and I became separated at this point, why, I can't remember, but, strangely, we met again at *King Alfred*; he had not made any effort to miss the draft to *Naiad* so, perhaps, my manoeuvres had been unnecessary.

It will be remembered that shortly before *Curlew* was hit I had removed my wristwatch. Having learned that about the one personal possession for which a rating could claim was his watch off I went to the

84

Pay Master's office and had a conversation, something like the following, with a CPO Writer.

> ME: "I lost my watch when *Curlew* was sunk."
> CPO: "You are a survivor?"
> ME: "Yes."
> CPO: "Your name and number."
> ME: "H. J. Messer AB, LDX 3771 London Division RNVR."
> CPO: Turning over pages — "You were part of the draft from HMS *President?*"
> ME: "Yes and no."
> CPO: "Ah, here is your name: H. J. Messer AB, LDX 3771."
> ME: "Yes."
> CPO: "What kind of a watch was it?"
> ME: "It was gold and a twenty-first birthday present."
> CPO: "What was it worth?"
> ME: "I am not sure but being gold it must have been fairly valuable."
> CPO: "About how valuable?"
> ME: "I should think about £50."
> CPO: "That is far too much."
> ME: "I don't think so, but how does £25 suit you?"
> CPO: "Still too much."

About now I was beginning to smell a rat but, nevertheless, pursued the rather one sided conversation.

> ME: "What would you like me to say?"
> CPO: "Ratings cannot claim more than £1 (it might have been £2) for a watch. Is that satisfactory?"
> ME: "Why didn't you tell me that in the first place? Then we could have avoided this charade!"
> CPO: No reply.

The forms were duly completed and I was instructed to return on the morrow. Then, I saw a young Sub/Lt. (Pay) who handed over the money. There was no point in remonstrating so I took the cash, signed the receipt and retreated as gracefully as I could.

It was at moments such as this that one realized the complete hopelessness of being on the lower deck; one was at the mercy of Naval procedure and anyone of senior rank empowered to augment that procedure. Moreover, one was brought face to face with the fact that, as an AB one had no right to own anything of value or, worse still, to be considered entitled to do so. When I became an officer and, more importantly, an officer in command of my own ship I tried to treat my crews as I had wished to be treated; their personal dignity was my first consideration.

My next draft was to the Naval Division (land fighting sailors); this was a surprise but not unwelcome as I associated the Division with commandos but how wrong I was. I found myself in a hut in the barracks together with a jolly pleasant GI and racks of rifles. My daily chore was to sit drinking tea with the GI and, occasionally, cleaning the rifles, Lewis-guns and other weapons. At least I had the opportunity to resume my peacetime recreation of rifle shooting.

The GI took the initiative and asked me whether I was happy in my work.

"This is no job for you," he remarked, "you are officer material and will never get a commission in this backwater."

So, he arranged for me to be returned to general service and mighty grateful to him I was for I was beginning to stagnate. Then came a period of illness and idleness until, finally, I joined Coastal Forces.

An uncle who had been in the First World War and had volunteered for the Army once again was stationed at Woolwich. He had a flat there which was convenient for me when I had all night leave despite it being on the top floor of its block and situated in a much bombed area. I was there on the night of the great fire blitz on the dock area of London; in fact I stood with my uncle and aunt on the flat roof watching the inferno. Later, after consuming a flagon of port and the greater part of a Stilton cheese we turned in. In the morning I was up very early to return to Chatham and, on leaving the block, to my horror I saw that the building opposite had been destroyed by a land mine during the night. Thanks to the port I had not heard a thing!

The journey back to Chatham was fraught with problems; no trains were running from Woolwich so, after a long walk and several buses I arrived at Lewisham. There was an air raid in progress at the time and, after sighting several Nazi planes the driver and conductor of the bus I was in at that moment abandoned their charge to seek shelter. With several other sailors I was obliged to disembark but not before we gave the crew the sharp edges of our tongues. Walking to the station we heard the most terrifying roar over our heads and dived smartly to the deck with our hands over the back of our necks; the roar continued at a steady rate and, looking up, we saw we were under a railbridge upon which was a slowly moving train!

Trains were running from Lewisham despite the falling bombs so, after a most unpleasant and nerve-racking journey, I joined the queue checking into the barracks.

Transport from all over the country had been disrupted causing the Regulating Petty Officer at the gate to be greeted as follows by the returning matelots:

RATING: "03.00 from Manchester, six hours late."
RPO: "OK."
RATING: "Midnight from Norwich, five hours late."
RPO: "OK."

and so on until the rating in front of me, who appeared to be a new entry by the way in which he wore his uniform, said:

"Have to be honest, Chief, afraid I overslept."
RPO: "Overslept! You ... ... words fail me, can't you think of a better yarn than that you ... ... Christ all bleeding mighty you're in the rattle for being such a ... ... Name and number."
ME: "No trains from Woolwich RPO."
RPO: "OK."

At night all those who were not on watch were obliged to sleep in the 'tunnels' as the air raid shelters were called. They were, indeed, tunnels hewn out of the chalk beneath the barracks. Normally, if not on watch I slept ashore or occupied myself in such a manner as to allay any suspicion. However, one night I was persuaded by a friend to go down and for my pains I caught scabies, a most unpleasant disease. This meant three weeks in hospital feeling anything but ill but very itchy; life there consisted of being treated with ointments and doing the hospital's domestic work. As well as assisting to clean the ward I was given the job of looking after the fires in the doctors' rooms. Why they needed fires in the middle of summer I shall never know, but each morning I would clean the grates and lay and light the fires. As most of the doctors were young and RNVR this was quite a congenial occupation for I had many long and interesting discussions with them on a variety of subjects.

When out of hospital never again did I venture down to the ghastly tunnels; normally, when in Chatham I slept at the Sailors' Rest for, if I

87

remember correctly, 1/- per night. It meant clean sheets, a single room, privacy and was well worth the outlay. In barracks I found somewhere quiet and out of reach of authority.

All this time the Battle of Britain was being fought overhead; in the barracks we had a grandstand view and would cheer when we saw Germans baling out from their stricken planes. On the other hand, I remember seeing one of our pilots being machine-gunned as he dangled, defenceless, from his parachute.

Soon after my leave had ended my brother was moved from Yorkshire to Colchester; he came and spent a night or two in Chatham and, later, I went up to Essex and we had a pleasant weekend together at the Red Lion hotel. These were the first occasions on which we had met since our call-up; needless to say we had much to discuss and rejoiced at our both being spared.

In barracks I made an assortment of friends, one of whom was a leading seaman whose parents lived in Chatham; his father was a dockyard matey, a species for whom I had little time until I met this one. Usually, I found them to be lazy, morose and only too eager to spin out their work regardless of the consequence. However, this chap was scornful of those of his mates who did not give of their best and was patriotic to a degree. I was invited back to the house, a two up and two downer in a terrace, on several occasions and each time I was given a jolly good supper and made to stay the night sharing a bed with my new friend. They were very kind folk and I am sure that I was eating their scanty rations. I took them what I could buy without a ration card but it was very little.

Another amusing character was an Irish able seaman who had been the cox'n of a submarine; I knew that he had been disrated but didn't like to ask him for the details. However, one night after a few beers he opened up. The ship had returned to Chatham after a particularly hazardous and gruelling patrol. "Suddenly, I felt that I had to hit some bastard," he said in his deep Irish brogue, "so I went up to the bridge and hit the Skipper who was the only bastard up there." My first reaction was to ask if the Skipper really had been a bastard. "Good Lord no," he replied, "the best Skipper I've ever served with." There is no understanding the Irish! I heard somewhere later that it had not been long before he had regained his old rank.

A messmate, a rather reserved and not too bright AB, asked me if I would go with him to Richmond where his father had been in the Star and Garter Home since the end of the First World War. Having obtained special leave off we went. It was not a pleasant experience to see those poor men, many of whom were so badly wounded that they had not left the home since their arrival. The AB's father was one of them; his face was not that of a normal man and to sit and talk with him — he could only mumble — required considerable self-control. I was glad to leave but felt very guilty at feeling glad.

An elderly three-badge AB wanted to run a raffle in the block and asked me if I would finance it, splitting the profits on a 50/50 basis. After learning how it would operate I agreed; all was quite simple in that we would buy large and attractive prizes from Goldbergs, display them in the mess, advertise the raffle throughout the block, *Hawke*, and beyond, sell tickets, have a grand draw and repeat the procedure. It all worked as my partner had foreseen; we ran several more successful raffles until the old fellow was drafted.

Other sailors wanted to continue with me but I had found a girl-friend ashore. She was in the ATS and was the daughter of a famous surgeon also well known as an after-dinner speaker. I took her out whenever our leaves coincided and visited her parents' house several times. Like most wartime romances it fizzled out when she was moved away from Chatham.

On most Sundays I would attend church parade, for it was pleasant to shift into No.1s and feel clean and relaxed with no work to do. But, on this particular Sabbath I had other ideas. The drill was that 'we all got fell in' and then C of Es were 'fell out' followed by the RCs, Baptists, Methodists et al. Finally, only two of us were left and, oddly, we were 'fell in' next to each other. The Chief GI turned to me.

"What are you for God's sake?"

"Jewish Chief."

"And you?" to the other chap.

"Jewish too Chief."

The CPO thought for a moment; this, obviously, was the first time in which he had been confronted with so strange a problem. At last, he bellowed, "Aint'cha got more respect for your religion? You're 'Ebrews aint'cha?"

"Yes chief?"

More thought then, "There ain't no sinigogs 'ere."

"No Chief."

A long silence and then a look of relief crossed his face, "You're IMCUDPARTY, follow me."

We looked at each other and, without any idea why, we followed him and soon discovered that we were to be the hymn card party when we were presented with a bundle of cards which we distributed along the lines of C of Es 'fell in' for the service. When finished our time was our own.

My new friend's name was similar to mine, in fact his started with the same syllable; he was in a different block but as kindred spirits (he was hoping for a commission) we sought each other's company whenever possible. We concocted a plan and wondered if we could deceive authority with a little bit of audacity, so we acquired signal pads and pencils and put the plan into operation. For three days we walked around the barracks purporting to check any windows broken by bomb blast; when challenged we replied that we were acting on behalf of the Commander and were never rumbled in our self-allotted task. We were given the 'run of the place' and received help from everyone we approached even being invited into the wardroom and other officers' quarters. At last it became tedious and, moreover, dangerous to continue so we consigned our findings to a gash bin and retired. While it lasted it was great fun. Eventually, we got so bored with doing nothing, neither of us seemed to be favourites with the drafting office, that we decided to do a gunnery course. After the usual formalities we were given permission and, eventually, both passed with 100% marks and became ABs QR3; our full titles being Able Seamen Quarters Ratings Third Class which, apart from having a certain but not very important standing where gunnery was concerned, meant, far more importantly, an extra few pence (was it ninepence?) per day in our pay packets. It served me well, also, in Coastal Forces as will be seen. The GI who took the course was a sweet old man — much too old for sea service — who was overjoyed to have in his class two intelligent ratings who were genuinely interested in what he had to say. I am afraid that we ragged him a bit but he got his own back by asking us to illustrate an old time punishment which entailed carrying a six-inch shell around the parade ground. He asked us in such a guileless manner to assist him in the illustration that it was not before we were on our way, laden down, that we realized how we had been duped.

Shortly after this my friend was drafted and I was on my own again. Another short friendship was with a chap whose family had a piano manufacturing business. One day I went with him on a nostalgic journey to see the remains of their bombed out factory which was in either Old Kent or Walworth Road; it was a sad occasion for him.

Some time around the end of the summer an AFO asked for volunteers for Coastal Forces; the signal was given a prominent place on the

Drill Shed notice-board. This seemed to me to be my kind of war so after a brief chat with the training officer, Lt. Guy Fison RNVR, I was in.

I was now recommended for a commission and had an interview with the Commander who deemed it to be necessary for me to go back to sea. It was obligatory to have an 'excellent' conduct rating which I had not been given from *Curlew*. This was most disappointing for I had done nine months' sea time, three more than the statutory requirement of six. Moreover, the main reason why so few of the RNVRs in *Curlew* had become CW candidates was, surely, because of the ineptness of the RNVR officers all of whom were trying to be more pusser than pusser; there is nobody more intolerant than one who does not know his job and there is no doubt that those officers were far from efficient so, consequently, to a man they lacked the confidence to act in a proper manner to the ratings in their charge. I had very little feeling for any of them.

Guy Fison, whom I have remet quite recently and who must have recommended me, confirmed that I was a CW candidate and expressed the opinion that I would need to do only the bare six months at sea. He and I got on well together; partly, I suppose, because he wanted to give me experience in handling men and, partly, because I was one of the few ABs on the course, he would put me in charge whenever no leading seaman was present.

I cannot remember much about the training except that it was pretty basic. Most of the other 'volunteers' were either new entry HO ordinary seamen or junior RN ratings who thought that they were on to a soft number. There were, of course, other gunnery ratings, torpedomen and WT operators; the cox'ns were RN leading seamen or Petty Officers. Each boat carried a PO motor mechanic, a leading stoker and one or two stokers but they all trained separately. I have a feeling that the cox'ns had their own course. I was the only RNVR and, in all my five years service in Coastal Forces I don't remember another RNVR rating. Although, latterly, at reunions I have met several.

The training lasted several weeks; I returned to gunnery school to swot up on the Lewis-gun (first stripped at school) and to learn the drill for the three-pounder.

Despite my new found enthusiasm for the course there was still the dreary barrack mess in the evenings. One small blessing was that each block had a reading room where talking was strictly prohibited and strictly enforced by the duty leading seaman. The room was starkly furnished with wooden tables and forms but for me it was an oasis in an arid desert of nescience and insensibility. Whenever not on duty or ashore I could be found there scribbling sonnets, writing letters or reading. Unfortunately, all the poetry which I wrote in Chatham has been lost; some of it, I was told, was quite reasonable.

To be able to remove myself from the noise and uncouthness of the mess deck was bliss.

During one of my trips to the Smoke (London) I met a Stornoway T124 rating on the train. He was a large, rough and tough character who sipped rum from a small bottle during the journey from Chatham. At Victoria both of us went to spend a penny; in the lavatory at the bottom of the steps we were accosted by a 'brown-hatter' (ponce); my companion's answer was to flatten him with a most savage blow and, almost before the poof's body had hit the deck, his wallet was in the trawlerman's vast hands. Giving me a wad of notes with a grunted, "'Ere's your share," he disappeared up the steps. Thinking discretion to be the better part of valour I returned the notes to the unconscious body and beat a hasty retreat before anyone should find me in that uncompromising situation. In fact, I didn't feel safe until I had left the station well behind me.

During my spell in Chatham I had two lucky escapes in incidents both of which could have had me picking oakum instead of going, eventually, to KA. The first occurred when leaving barracks for weekend leave. I had been asked by friends ashore if it was possible to obtain some pipe tobacco and, extremely unwisely, I had said yes to the request and, even more unwisely, had considered it necessary to fulfil my promise. Normally, leaving the barracks was a formality, one nodded to the Duty RPO, passed the time of day with him and went through the gate into the comparative freedom of civvy street. Beguiled by the simplicity of it all naïvely I bought enough tobacco from willing messmates to fill one of the small brown attaché cases carried by sailors when on leave; I placed a towel over my contraband and headed for the main gate.

I was fully aware of the consequences of being caught smuggling tobacco, a very serious crime in the Navy then and, I have no doubt, now. What possessed me to embark on so foolish and risky an enterprise is beyond me, but I must have been lulled into a false sense of security by the previous lack of real discipline at the gate. So, my consternation can be imagined when I realized that on this occasion all cases were being examined. My first reaction was to retreat, but noticed that Petty Officers had been placed in strategic positions to circumvent this escape route. There was nothing to do but brazen it out so, having put a £1 note on the towel I advanced to the gate; my heart was beating, my pulses were throbbing and I was sweating with apprehension. 'Surely,' I thought, 'I must look guilty.' When requested to do so I half opened the case towards the PO, a hand came out and took the £1, a peaked cap nodded to me and I was through. Lady Luck was with me; my friends could not have appreciated how near to disaster I had come in satisfying their needs.

The other situation developed one day when I was cook of the mess. All the lower deck galleys in the barracks were situated beneath the messes at the bottom of each block, so down I went to collect the food; while doing so I was offered some butter by one of the cooks. "Take it home to your mum, Lofty." While considering whether to accept, the butter was placed on the tray; cries from behind of, "Chop chop Lofty" sent me on my way back to the mess still in possession of that butter. My adventure with the tobacco had taught me a lesson so I presented the pack to the killick, a wise old leading hand, who ordered me to return it to the galley. On my return he lectured me about the dangers of Greeks bearing gifts, but not, I would add, in classical terms.

The Coastal Force training was carried out in the dockyard and, for transporting heavy loads, we had a lorry which we could call on; I was one of the drivers. Some time after the offer of butter I was asked, point blank, whether I would take some sides of bacon to a house in the town; there was, of course, the bribe of a substantial pay-off. I refused, there was never any likelihood of my having agreed to do it although my persuaders did not easily give up. A few days later the whole operation was blown sky high when a supply CPO's house, close to the barracks, was raided and found to be stacked from floor to ceiling, in every room, with stolen stores. This was the address to which I had been asked to take the bacon; "Only a very short trip, Lofty."

Senior and junior officers together with senior and junior ratings were all involved in the swindle which I understand extended to Portsmouth and Devonport. Their organization must have been thorough for them to have known of my brief association with the lorry.

At the end of the course I was drafted to HMML 103, an early A-type boat which was based at Chatham. She was commanded by a charming but not too seamanlike Lt. RNVR; the boat was run by the cox'n, a most efficient and experienced leading seaman with whom I got on well and from whom I learned a great deal. As the gunnery rating I was next in seniority on the upper deck to him and, together, we kept the ML 'shipshape and Bristol fashion.' The guns, of course, were my responsibility.

I remember an MTB coming alongside (I think that it was 102 the training boat) and the CO inviting us to go for a spin. I did so and from that moment my ambition was to command one. I was on the point of requesting a transfer when I discovered that MTB crews lived ashore in barracks; I'd had my fill of barracks so changed my mind. I was determined, however, that when I was commissioned I would serve in MTBs. My first impressions were of oil, speed, elan and lethality; I pictured myself on the bridge, ploughing through heavy seas, in a single handed attack on the entire German Fleet. In fact, a new Percy F. Westerman adventure, *A Sub and an MTB*.

A Zeebrugge type of operation was in the offing and we were to be part of it. To this end we made several trips down to Gravesend where the Headquarters Ship was moored in the stream; she was earmarked for the blockship as well and we, so the buzz informed us, were to take the senior officers off her when she was in position. Buzzes on the lower deck were notoriously unreliable; I, for one, hoped that this one was false.

On our final visit we managed to tangle our mast in the HQ ship's davits and, in endeavouring to extricate ourselves we damaged our hull. I was on the wheel, in the wheelhouse, so didn't appreciate what had happened until we were disentangled and moored alongside.

Worse was to follow for on the way back upstream we ran aground; when the tide receded we were left, like a stranded whale, high up in the mud on the right bank. How we got there is beyond my comprehension, but I did hear that the CO was given a job ashore after the débâcle.

While there was still some water the cox'n, who had taken charge, managed, with my help, to lay out our bow anchor using the dinghy, but we had to finish securing the ML by sloshing about in the mud. The boat was a filthy mess as, indeed, were we all; we turned in for a few hours until the tide came up allowing us to be towed to Chatham where we set about cleaning the boat but our clothes were beyond redemption.

So, back to barracks and no glorious adventure with the blockship. It wasn't to matter for the operation was called off because of security; everyone in Chatham knew of it and so, I am sure, did the Germans.

Soon after, just before Christmas, I was drafted to HMML 147 building at Brooke's Yard, Lowestoft.

A young sparker, who had been in the training unit and who, also, was joining 147, came to me for advice and a loan. He had requested all night leave so that he might say goodbye to his parents, but had been told at the drafting office that it would cost him 10/-. The poor lad was in a pathetic state for the payment of the demand would not leave him enough for his leave. I accompanied him back to the office where the Danegeld was confirmed so I handed over £1 in order that both of us could go. I was furious and, in some manner which I cannot recall, made this extortion public and like to think that, in some small way, I was responsible for its break-up for broken up it was. Later, I was glad to hear the Drafting Master-at-Arms had been disrated and sent to sea as were all his henchmen. Some strange stories emerged from the subsequent enquiry, one of which was that the Commodore's gardener had been in barracks for the previous seventeen years! I wondered how he enjoyed his return to sea.

On Christmas Eve 1940 the crew of HMML 147 arrived in Lowestoft where the ratings spent the next few nights in digs. I remember, on turning in that night, hearing gunfire coming from seaward and thinking, 'Here we go again!'

Chapter 7

When a matelot moved he did so rather like a Romany, taking his possessions with him. His hammock (sailors no longer sleep in them) was an issue for which he had to sign and for which he was responsible; his personal possessions were stowed in his kitbag. So, on the morning of Christmas Eve 1940 I, with the other members of the crew of HMML 147 'got fell in' with 'bags and 'ammicks' outside the Drafting Master-at-Arm's office in Chatham barracks. We were taken under the wings of a very young and immature Canadian Sub Lt. RCNVR who set our course for Lowestoft. I cannot remember much about the journey but I do have a vivid memory of the cox'n and I sculling around Fenchurch Street, burdened down by our kitbags and hammocks; what we were doing boarding and disembarking from buses in that thoroughfare is long forgotten.

The cox'n, 'Nick' Carter was the best type of RN sailor, he and I hit it off immediately. He was short and fairish and had been confirmed, very recently, as a leading hand. He worked hard to prosecute the war, was never missing nor, perhaps more important, at a loss during a crisis; if anything, he was a little too easy going in his approach to discipline but as 147 was a pretty efficient boat that criticism might be a bit hard. I liked him. He lived at Reading and, as my parents had by now moved to a furnished house in Maidenhead, we travelled together on the one occasion on which leave was granted. On the way he came to our house just when my mother was giving a small party and charmed all those present.

If I had been obliged to remain on the lower deck for the duration of the war (a thought which gave me the shudders whenever I contemplated it) I would, on reflection, have chosen to do so in 147. As well as having a decent CO, Lt. D. Wilkie RNVR, and cox'n, life on board a small boat was quite congenial. I was responsible for the guns, such as they were, and was in charge of the upper deck acting as a very small-time bo'sun. I did all the splicing and all the chores which might be classified under the heading of seamanship; indeed, it was rather like having my own yacht for, on the whole, I did what I thought was necessary while working, by and large, to my own routine. With the cox'n on the wheel the foredeck was my responsibility at sea and when entering or leaving harbour. All in all, it was 'messing about in boats' in wartime.

I was fortunate in my CO for, as far as it is possible for such a relationship to develop between rating and officer, Wilkie and I formed a companionship based, at least from my stand point, on a liking and respect. We spent hours together on the bridge during our sea-time, especially while on East Coast convoy duty. It was then, mostly at night, that we exchanged confidences despite Wilkie's inbuilt reticence.

Lt. David Wilkie RNVR was a quiet, unobtrusive, unflamboyant and reserved man in his early thirties. Never did he push himself forward, a trait which, unfortunately, he was apt to exercise to the detriment of others. He was a fine seaman, a good navigator, dogged to a degree and, to my knowledge and while I was with him, never shirked his duty. Usually, he prefaced his orders to me with, "Would you mind, Messer...." He was obstinate and durable but if he had a major fault and, being human he was not faultless, it was that he did not assert himself strongly enough, often enough and quickly enough. He was not a great leader nor a great mixer and was, perhaps, happiest when operating on a detached command as he was for most of the time I was with him.

The 1st Lt. was a Canadian Sub. Lt. RCNVR; he was tall, ungainly, extremely likeable but of not much help to his CO. He was indecisive, inexperienced, slow to learn and clumsy in mind as well as body. He had enormous feet and was constantly stumbling about the boat. We heard, after he left us, that he had fallen over the side, during a battle, and was lost. He exasperated me but I liked him and always endeavoured to help him if I could; I was sad when I heard of his death.

The remainder of the crew were the cook, a taciturn Hostilities Only Yorkshireman who had been a cutter at Burtons in Leeds; the torpedo-man and the trained man, both active service RN and not up to much (very strange for RN ratings; perhaps they needed tighter discipline); a very young sparker, also Hostilities Only, who kept very much to himself and who, later, signed on for his twelve. Their approach to the war was so different from the RNVRs in *Curlew*; they did as little as possible and skived whenever the opportunity presented itself (except, perhaps, the cook). At sea they did their watch (on the messdeck if they could) and that was it. If I had been the 1st Lt. they would have had me on their tails.

There were three in the engine-room, the motor mechanic, the leading stoker and a stoker. The MM, a Petty Officer, was a delightful garage owner from Beccles who had the broadest and most musical Norfolk burr; he was good both at his job and as a sobering influence on the messdeck. Incidentally, we all messed together but the cox'n and MM shared a two berth sleeping cabin. The leading stoker I remember for his good looks, his jolly nature and his extreme cleanliness; whatever work he undertook on his engines he emerged spotless in his faded blue overalls with their white badges of rank. On one occasion, when going to action stations, he slipped on the engine-room ladder, caught his ring on a projection and pulled his right middle finger out at the knuckle joint. The next morning, on our return to Lowestoft, he went to hospital together with his finger and we did not see him again; he was a loss to the boat. I forget, quite completely, his successor. The stoker was a young lad, no different from any other lively youngster, who was up to all kinds of mischief, always on the search for a willing 'party' when ashore and full of beer and his imagined conquests when back on board; he kept us amused and was well liked. The engine-room complement were as keen and efficient as the upper deck ratings were lazy and inefficient.

It has to be admitted that most of the crew treated me with suspicion for they knew that I was a CW candidate, very little can be kept secret on the messdeck; besides the cox'n only the MM and the leading stoker were at all friendly, the remainder, although far from hostile, were not as warm as they might have been. Perhaps, an additional factor was that I was on Wilkie's side in wishing to prosecute the war as fiercely as possible and, also, to make 147 as efficient as possible to carry out that purpose. The situation was exacerbated by my being thrust, most unwillingly, into the cox'n's place whenever he was ashore; hence, I was obliged to give orders to chaps who were on the same level but, probably, what rankled among the crew, was that this authority could be exercised, only, through the backing of the two officers.

All the differences of social position and education were far more apparent in so small a ship than they had been in *Curlew* where those factors were hidden beneath an earnest and shared desire to get on with things. Added to all this was the plain fact that, apart from the cox'n, I was, by far, the most competent hand in every aspect of seamanship and this riled the two RN ratings to an extreme causing them to stir things up among the others. It was rather like being teacher's pet in a kinder-garten. On reflection, maybe I wasn't, always, too tactful.

Motor launches were on canteen messing which meant that with careful management we could live well and within our allowance. The cooks of the mess drew the basic food and any extras from NAAFI. There is no doubt that we did not want in 147, we lived plainly but well; we were not venturesome nor extravagant but there was plenty, always, at each meal.

The crews of MLs were entitled to extra pay, called 'hard-lying money', because service in small boats was considered more uncomfortable than in larger ships. This astounded me for my time in 147 was, by far, the most comfortable of my two years on the lower deck. Able seamen were paid about 1/- extra per day and this, together with gunnery and rate pay made me reasonably well off. We did so much sea time that the very infrequent runs ashore were the sole expense. Beer was cheap. we ate most of our meals on board and, rarely, ashore so the drain on our pockets was far from heavy. Anyway there was little to do in Lowestoft, the pubs were pretty dreary and full of trawlermen so an occasional visit to the pictures sufficed. Normally, I was content to stay on board writing letters, reading or working on the boat. While we were on the East Coast Convoy run sleep was the first essential and all other attractions lost their glitter.

As an adjunct to hard-lying money we were issued with oiled wool sweaters and seaboot stockings which were a boon during the winter months at sea.

In those early days of Coastal Forces at Lowestoft the base, HMS *Mantis*, catered solely for the M/S trawlers. There were no showers or recreational facilities, when we needed a bath the cox'n and I would go to a nearby hotel (The London?) which was soon to be bombed and destroyed, where we would expend sixpence each on cleanliness.

Very shortly after we had commissioned I was walking past a trawler in the Fish Dock when a rating, who was doing his dhobying in a bucket on the foredeck, engaged me in conversation.

"You off them motor boats Lofty?"

"Yes."

"I reckon you got a soft number."

"Yes."

"Do you dhobi your socks?"

"Why?"

"See these 'ere."

The trawlerman held up his feet which were encased in a pair of filthy socks through which poked ten far from clean toes.

"Don't dhobi mine, wear 'em till they're like these and then ditch 'em. Don't waste your time dhobying socks, Lofty."

I thanked him for his advice and continued on my way.

On another occasion my meeting with trawlermen was not so peaceful. One Sunday the cox'n and I were sailing the dinghy on Oulton Broad while, on the coaling wharf stood a couple of very drunk ratings hurling abuse at us. We were every kind of 'brown hatter' and, what is more, completely feminine for serving in MLs and, moreover, we were yellow bastards because we wouldn't go ashore and fight them. I was quite happy to let them continue to exercise their jaw bones, 'sticks and stones can break my bones but names can never hurt me.' I had no wish to become involved in the sticks and stones because I knew that we would come off second best, but the cox'n was riled and his RN pride ruffled. I tried to talk him out of it but he was set on ramming their words down their throats so we steered for the wharf.

In the ensuing fight the valiant cox'n ended up in the drink and I face down with my nose being ground into the coal dust. When our assailants were satisfied, they were decent enough to acknowledge that we had put up a good enough fight for there to be handshakes all round. I do believe, to this day, that the other three enjoyed themselves.

147 was a B Class ML; she was a wooden, twin screw boat powered by a pair of 600 h.p. Hall Scott petrol engines which gave her a maximum speed of about 18 knots at 2,000 revs. Her dimensions were 112ft. x 18ft.3ins. x 3ft.8ins. forward and 4ft.9ins. aft; displacing 65 tons.

The living accommodation comprised the wardroom, heads and washbasins right aft and the messdeck, heads and washbasins right forward. The wardroom had four bunks, although only two officers were carried as normal complement, it was most comfortable and, indeed, spacious. The messdeck had six bunks arranged along each side, these, apart from the bottom ones, could be secured back against the bulkhead. The heads and washbasins were in the bows. Both wardroom and messdeck were heated by coal stoves. All the joinery work down below and in the wheelhouse was of the best workmanship, the varnished finish made one think of expensive yachts.

On the upper deck, from aft, were the depth charges, wardroom hatch, Holman Projector when fitted, the three-pounder, dinghy stowage, engine-room hatch, bridge and wheelhouse abaft of which was the messdeck hatch and, on the foredeck a hatch and the Lewis-gun which was replaced, in time, by the Bofors.

When we commissioned our main armament consisted of an old three-pounder, breech-loading, signalling gun dating from the nineteenth century and a stripped Lewis-gun as used in the 1914/18 war. Our secondary armament was the CO's revolver and some hand-grenades for throwing at the enemy! Later, we were fitted with a Holman Projector which was quite useless and, later still, with a Bofors upon which I doted.

Forward of the messdeck on the port side was the cox'n and MM's cabin while to starboard was the galley which contained a coal-fired range.

The engine-room and petrol tanks, which were self-sealing and carried 2,300 gallons, were amidships between the living accommodation.

We were expected to and, indeed, did engage German aircraft with the Lewis-gun and E-boats with the three-pounder. It was as well that we didn't get close enough to use the hand-grenades! Perhaps, a few of the pre-war appeasers and anti-rearmers should have been in our place.

The boat remained in the hands of the builders for many days after we had arrived so we continued to sleep in our billets. The cox'n and I shared a double bed in a tiny house where our situation was too dreadful for words. The bed was not just damp but positively wet; the owners of the house were uncouth, unfriendly, not too clean and utterly unfit to accommodate rats, let alone humans. As soon as it was possible to sleep on board we had Wilkie's special permission to do so and left that dump without a backward look.

It was no surprise that I developed bronchitis and had two days off duty with a very high temperature. I must have been fit in those days, perhaps, as fit as ever I have been, for I walked a good mile to the doctor while suffering a temperature of 104 degrees and then, after a short examination, walked all the way back to the boat. Reporting to Wilkie, on my return, I took the prescribed aspirin, dived for my bunk, slept and sweated for 48 hours and then got up, fully recovered, ready to ammunition ship.

There was a lot to do in commissioning a motor launch and much of it was new to us all. The 1st Lt. was not a great deal of help, Wilkie was busy with more important things so the responsibility fell to the cox'n who shouldered it well. With me as his mate, stores were accepted and stowed, faults reported to the builders and the bookwork completed. Sometimes, the latter baffled him when I was called to help and, together, we unravelled the system and hoped that our efforts would satisfy the paybobs.

The cox'n, besides, was employed in allocating work, drawing up routines and keeping an eye on the greener and/or more light-fingered members of the crew. He coped well.

During one of our deliberations I found that it was possible to perpetrate a swindle with regard to the rum ration. I forget how it worked but it concerned those ratings who didn't draw and those who were under age and unable to draw. The plan could be activated in only the first few weeks of the commission and it worked for, at the end of the prescribed period, we had a healthy surplus which those of us who drew drank one Saturday lunch-time. It was ferocious stuff for in MLs the rum issue was neat unlike that in general service where it was mixed with water.

After several hours sleep the cox'n and I went ashore to the local dance hall where the first drink started us off all over again. My companion told the band leader that I was a famous London crooner who wished to remain incognito; before I could protest I found myself on the stage, before a mike facing a sea of yelling matelots and their girl-friends. The leader announced me with a great flourish of the brass and a strident roll of the drums. 'Hell and damn it,' I thought, 'they can but howl me down,' which is exactly what they did.

Diverting for a moment it has to be told that the leading stoker, who went ashore before us, woke up the next morning and remembered absolutely nothing of the previous twelve hours, not even drinking his rum.

Leaving the dance hall was a safety measure which I considered to be prudent; the cox'n had met a party and had to be prised away. We made our way to the docks and played trains with the goods wagons; being joined by several other sailors we shunted the wagons and had great fun. Abandoning that pursuit at the approach of authority we found a bus which we drove round the town dropping off the passengers at their own front doors. How we managed to gain possession of that bus is lost in the past, but I do remember that we had the full support of the public both on and off the vehicle. By God's grace we returned to 147 undetected, or so we thought; however, the next morning one of the COs in the flotilla with whom I was on good terms, called me over to his boat. He warned me that the description of the 'wanted men' resembled the cox'n and myself.

"I know it was you," said the officer, "because I saw you. Keep silent and don't boast of your exploit and it will blow over. You can rely on me not to split on you."

I thanked him, returned to 147 and told the cox'n who, having no wish to lose his hook, kept very quiet. In a few days the whole thing had been forgotten. We were very lucky or, perhaps, authority was on our side. There cannot have been many combinations of a tall, dark RNVR able seaman and a short fair leading seaman in Lowestoft. I am sure Wilkie knew that we were the culprits.

Apart from assisting the cox'n my main job, other than the guns and ammunition, during the commissioning period was the preparation of the warps, heaving lines, fenders, lead lines, anchor cables, and all the ancillary upper deck gear. In this I was guided by a Chief Buffer, too old for sea, who was attached to the base for this purpose, he acted as instructor and mentor to raw sailors such as I was. We spent hours together on the foredeck perfecting my splicing and general knots; then he taught me a variety of fancy knots as well as how to splice wire. He was a natural teacher and when he had finished with me I was reasonably able. In time 147 was full of Turk's heads and similar decorations; they were on stanchions, ladders, the dinghy's oars and, in fact, wherever a fancy knot was appropriate one was to be seen. They were not all as tiddley as they might have been but they gave me satisfaction.

At last we were ready for sea and, after acceptance trials, we did a few days working up which, as far as I was concerned, consisted of firing the three-pounder at and hitting a towed target as well as testing the Lewis-gun and revolver.

There were not many MLs in Lowestoft at that time and, perhaps, more importantly there were very few with experienced skippers. We, Lt. Fanner in 145 and one other were the exceptions and in much demand. It would have been inappropriate if we had been branded as, 'jolly good lads in harbour' for we were seldom there; the second line might have suited, 'But oh my Christ at sea.'

Our first task was as part of the escort to a very big mine-laying operation off the Dutch coast in which quite a few ships were involved all under the command of a Commander RN. It was the first time, at sea, that I knew what was happening; the chart was open in the wheelhouse with our positions marked on it, Wilkie had briefed us and common sense filled in the gaps. One of the plusses of service in small craft, as a rating, was that the crew were seldom in the dark regarding operations; seldom is repeated for sometimes the chart was not available and no amount of questioning would elicit a reply. We could, of course, watch the compass and surmise.

Before we had sailed from Lowestoft we took on board a trawler skipper to assist in the navigation which, of necessity, had to be precise. I am not certain after all this time but I believe that each vessel taking part in the operation had been allocated a skipper, at least all the escorting MLs carried one. It is an understatement to record that Wilkie was not pleased with the arrangement.

When in position we split up with orders to reassemble at a certain position and time. Our job was as guardship to the Western Wing of the Squadron although what we could have done, if attacked, was both laughable and pathetic. The Gods must have been with us for, immediately, a thick mist came down; I can remember the feeling of utter loneliness as we wallowed, with engines stopped, in that grey, heaving wilderness within a few hundred yards of the Dutch coast listening to the sounds of voices from the shore. I stood, with my gun's crew, beside the loaded three-pounder wondering how that primitive weapon would deter even a rowing boat. Talking and smoking were prohibited on the upper deck while all movements were carried out by only those wearing rubber soled boots; down below all lights, even in the engine-room, were extinguished. The wheelhouse was blacked out and the only lights were those on the compass and over the chart table and they were so dim as to be visible only from right above. At last, came the time to move for the rendezvous which we did at dead slow ahead but the sound of the engines sounded like thunder. 'If we could hear their voices ashore,' I thought, 'then surely, they must be able to hear us.' But nothing happened, the expected gunfire did not materialize as we proceeded on the prearranged course for Lowestoft.

Our trawler skipper was an enormously fat man who was famous both in the North and Irish Seas. I was on the bridge when we moved, the 1st Lt. having taken over at the gun.

"Can you use a lead?" asked the skipper.

"Yes," I replied, though I had not heaved a lead line other than in practice. The cox'n was on the wheel in the wheelhouse while Wilkie was laying off the course for home. Up top the skipper made one or two disparaging remarks concerning the SO of the operation in particular, and RN officers in general and then ordered a new course down the voice pipe. Up came our CO, full of wrath, but the fat man must have had some authority given to him for he just ignored Wilkie. Then, turning to me he asked if we had tallow on board and if so would I load the lead. This I did and was positioned by the guardrail on the starboard side of the bridge. I was ordered to take the lead to the skipper after each 'heave' when he examined what was sticking to the tallow and was then able to ascertain the bottom. Distinctly, do I remember when we crossed Brown Ridge the fat man's grunt of satisfaction as the bottom indicated that we were on course. At that moment so thick had the fog become that our bow was only just visible from the bridge.

We passed smack between the two breakwaters which form the entrance to Lowestoft's harbour, the first back by some time. Dawn had broken but it was still very thick. All the old skipper had used besides his local knowledge and experience were the compass and lead line — he had not looked once at the chart; even Wilkie was impressed.

Continually and especially over Brown Ridge which is fairly shallow, he had been pointing out to me the different colours of the sea and how the depth, or conversely the shallowness, affected the shape of the waves.

I do not know whether anything was said about our wilfully disobeying orders but, in that fog, it would not have been easy to prove although the main force did, on the whole, stick together.

When we were secured alongside I asked the skipper how he did it. "Now, well," he replied, "every quarter has a distinct smell so when the wind is blowing from that direction all I have to do is take a fix with this." He tapped his nose and, with a wink, left the bridge saying, "I smell my way."

Lowestoft was bombed repeatedly by sneak raiders who came in under cover of the sun usually over the timber merchants, Jewson's warehouse. It was always at mealtimes that the sirens would sound; off I would go to man the Lewis-gun which was as much good as a pea-shooter fending off a tank, the arrogance of those Nazis got my goat. How I longed for a decent gun and how those Germans must have chuckled at our pathetic defences. There was an AA battery in the vicinity, but it was not much of a deterrent nor were the barrage balloons but, worst of all, neither were the guns on the trawlers and MLs in the harbour. After dropping their bombs, almost at will, the planes would depart virtually unharmed and we would return to our ruined meal. I repeat, it got my goat.

After the mine-laying exercise we were directed to the East Coast Convoy run. Owing to the necessity for coastal shipping in the North Sea to keep to established and well buoyed channels, our convoys were particularly vulnerable to attack by aircraft and E-boats; in fact, the Germans had but to sit and wait for the easy pickings to arrive. Those convoys had to be well protected and MLs were part of the escort.

Soon we had settled into a routine with Lt. Fanner; we commenced by going north and then when we came south he went north and this we kept up for many weeks. It was exhausting for we would leave Lowestoft in the evening, join and stay with the convoy until morning when we would go into Immingham, there we would spend the day returning with the southbound convoy that night. I forget how many times this was repeated before we had a spell in harbour to recuperate but it was very many and the break was for but twenty-four hours.

In harbour, during the morning, I would clean the guns and square up the upper deck before a shave and a shower. After dinner it was a case of cracking my swede down until the late afternoon when we sailed. It was, indeed, exhausting.

The first morning on which we returned to Lowestoft from Immingham there was an air raid while I was cleaning the guns. Not yet too confident I reassembled the Lewis-gun in haste only to find that, when finished, I had a part left over. With Wilkie's "Come on Messer" and the cox'n's "Chop Chop Lofty" I didn't think it wise to admit my error so I slapped on a pan of ammunition and, to my utter surprise, the gun fired and kept on doing so. The part was safely stowed in my pocket so, when the panic was over, I cleaned the gun and reassembled it with the recalcitrant part in place. When I told the tale to the cox'n he didn't believe me or more strictly, didn't believe that it was possible. Anyway, I didn't attempt to prove that it was.

When at sea I would spend the night on the bridge with interruptions only for my tricks on the wheel. The other all-nighter was the cox'n who kept a weather eye on everything. The remainder of the upper deck crew stood their watches but beetled off to their bunks immediately they were relieved.

It was during the long night watches that the strange bond between Wilkie and I developed. He would be sitting, wedged into the starboard corner of the bridge while I stood in the centre. As we got to know each other better so the more intimate our conversations became. On reflection, both of us were in need of the other; I for the obvious reason that I welcomed talking to an equal and Wilkie, because he was marooned in the wardroom with a very young First Lt. with whom he had nothing in common. Admittedly, when in harbour he could seek the company of the other officers but he was a reserved man who didn't open up easily to strangers.

Oddly enough, I had a similar relationship with a rating when I was an officer and in command of a largish ship in India. He was an American signalman, a graduate of Harvard University, who had joined the Royal Navy while in London when America entered the war. The unfortunate fellow had found it difficult not only to get off the lower deck but to obtain a transfer to the US Navy. I did what I could to help him and when I left the ship he was well on the way for his request to be granted. Most of the officers in that ship, HMS *Kedah*, were either very young or T.124; I had little in common with any of them, except the 2nd Engineer, so would talk to the American as Wilkie had talked to me.

During most of the early convoys the weather was abysmal. We would be doing, at the most, about eight knots and often much less, in freezing conditions and in heavy and diffused seas. An ML rolled most unpleasantly at slow speeds so that in the short seas to be encountered off England's east coast her movement was vigorous, uncomfortable and most tiring. After a short time exposed to hail, snow, freezing spray and icy solid water those on the bridge were soaked through and stiff with cold. As the boat pitched into the white capped, curling waves cascades of salt water were hurled at the bridge, we became adept at premeditating the enforced bath but ducking below the dodger merely avoided the main mass of water; its tributaries had an uncanny knack of finding any weakness in our waterproof clothing to trickle down and become absorbed by our gradually sodden underclothes. In an emergency we were obliged to stand straight and accept each wave full in the face, wipe away the spray from our eyes and wait for the next wave. Repeated cups of soup, cocoa, tea or Bovril helped to reduce the misery.

During the periods of daylight we were under near constant attack from enemy planes and, at night, by E-boats. With our pathetic armament we could do little, if anything, in the protection of the convoys; often, I wondered why we were there. Ships would be crippled and sunk but ever onwards sailed the lumbering merchantmen, yawing, pitching and rolling as they pushed their clumsy, ungainly way north or south resembling nothing more than great primeval giants of limited intelligence struggling for life in a devilish vortex. An incongruous addition to the scene was the ludicrous sight of the barrage balloons growing from some of the ships.

The convoys had little, if any, air cover so the escorts had to rely on their own guns for defence against air attack. The Admiralty had issued orders that any plane approaching a ship should be fired on if it did not reply to the challenge of the day, consequently more than a few of our own pilots suffered the indignity of attack from their own side. Very often it was their own fault for buzzing HM ships but there were occasions when, in the morning returning from a bombing raid tired and not sure of their position and too exhausted to alter course, inadvertently they would stray too close to the convoy and be obliged to suffer the consequences. After justified complaints from the RAF the order was rescinded. Again quite unfairly, for they had too many commitments and too few planes, the RAF was blamed for the convoys' exposure to the relentless Nazi air attacks.

One night towards dawn we were ordered to stand by a crippled merchantman and to take off her crew if they wished to abandon ship. It was snowing and a heavy sea was running in near gale conditions. When we met up with the casualty we found her to be well down by the head and listing to port, obviously she was not going to last much longer and the crew were gathered on her poop ready to be taken off. Owing to the wind direction and the wreck's condition we were obliged to approach her from her starboard quarter.

"Would you mind trying to get a line aboard her Messer, I will come up under her starboard quarter."

"Aye aye, Sir."

"I want plenty of fenders on our port bow and you will secure yourself with a life line. You have your lifebelt on?"

"Aye aye, Sir."

After the fenders had been secured:

"Do you want any help on the fo'c'sle?"

"I'd rather be on my own Sir."

"Very good. Then let's start the first run."

Immediately, I realized that we had a problem as I stood on the foredeck holding a heaving line watching the great black, rust stained, dripping, heaving mass of steel grow closer. The rudder was out of the water as was the screw; while we closed the noise reminded me of the sea rushing through a cave as the water surged around the wreck's stern. By now I was soaked, very cold and scared and could see no sense in securing the ML to that heaving mass. Fortunately, Wilkie was of the same opinion and ordered me to drop the heaving line.

As he backed away he shouted, "I'll have another go, tell them to jump when our bow is under their quarter."

The crew, gathered on the poop, also looked cold and scared. They appeared, in the half dark, to resemble the Michelin tyre advertisement in their ungainly, bulky life-jackets. Oddly, I could see no sign of any wounded; perhaps, there were none.

Forward we edged again and this time I touched the stricken ship as I shouted to the men to jump. Some shook their heads, some had a leg over the taffrail and then decided against it so we were obliged to back off. Again we closed and again nobody jumped; I suggested that they leap into the sea but that had no takers.

Each time that we had closed I expected the rudder to drive through our bow or the screw to rip us open; also, there was the fear of being knocked unconscious for I rose and fell alarmingly, one second level with the wreck's taffrail and looking into her crew's faces and the next I was under the dark of her counter. If Wilkie had miscalculated I would have been trapped.

"Do you think it might be better on her starboard side?"

"It's not so much of a jump for the crew Sir, I'll tell them what you intend to do."

"Thank you."

I shouted the new instructions to them as, once again, we closed; they trooped off the poop looking dispirited as they made their way forward. I thought that the best way out of their predicament was for their ship to sink and for us to pick them up out the sea.

"Right, Messer. I'll try to starboard."

Round we came and closed her abaft her forward well deck which was all but covered and being swept by waves which were surging, most dangerously, across her. I could see that it was possible for us to be carried on to the casualty and, besides, there were many projections which could easily have pierced our comparatively fragile, wooden hull so I shouted to Wilkie to go astern and get clear. As he did so I watched the heads of the crew drop in disappointment.

"I'll try again on her quarter."

"Aye aye, Sir."

Once again we edged under that fearsome, heaving stern but again to no avail. Then wonder of wonders, for as we backed off a lifeboat appeared on our port bow; it was, if I remember correctly, the Cromer boat. Her cox'n shouted that he would take over and asked me to request Wilkie to stand clear.

After a wave and a thank you from the crew we continued on our way to rejoin the convoy. A last look back revealed the men in a much happier frame of mind as the lifeboat manoeuvred alongside their sinking ship.

All the damage we had suffered was slight scoring to the gunwale and hull plus minimal bending of the port guardrails. Wilkie's handling of the ML, well supported by the cox'n on the wheel and engine telegraphs, had been exemplary. The engine-room's quick and efficient response to the telegraphs had played no small part in both mine and the boat's safety.

In all our many convoys we had but a single one to one engagement with an E-boat; nearly did I use the word battle but that would have flattered the meeting. The story is worth telling if only to illustrate our impotence and, also, for the farcical ending.

Smith's Knoll, a buoy, was where the E-boats would wait for the convoys; some maintained that they brought picnics with them, secured themselves to the buoy and enjoyed the ozone while they waited. It was in this position that we met our E-boat.

We were stationed at the southern end of a north bound convoy which had been under fierce attack and which had lost several ships sunk and more damaged; we had been at action stations for some time. I was on the three-pounder which, fortunately, was trained to starboard when a shout from Wilkie reported an E-boat fine on our starboard bow and on the reciprocal course to ours. Quickly, he turned to port to open the bearing so that I could see the quarry which was easily visible owing to the abundance of starshell being thrown up by the convoy's escorts. I fired once on sighting her, again when she was abeam and once more at her stern. All I could manage was those three miserable shells fired over an open sight from an unstable platform at a target travelling very fast. What a difference from the E-boat which, as she sped by a mere 50 feet away, swept us with her quick firing guns; as luck would have it she fired high and did us no harm whatsoever.

All was not gloom however, for I thought that our second shot was a hit — it should have been at that range — as did Wilkie and some of the crew. In the hope that our possible hit might slow her we turned to chase at our sedate 18 knots (E-boats were capable of more than twice that) and, very soon, came to a grinding halt on the Haisborough Sands where we stayed till morning. Not often did Wilkie lose his rag but, on this occasion, he went for the 1st Lt. tooth and nail; the poor chap had not come out of our short action too well (inefficiency not lack of courage) and now was in utter disgrace owing to his faulty navigation.

In attempting to refloat the ML we damaged one or both shafts and propellers as well as the starboard gearbox. All we could do was to anchor and wait for the tide.

A high sea was running and, although we had veered as much cable as was possible, we still snubbed against the anchor causing the pawl on the winch to carry away. When the boat was floating and we attempted to recover the anchor the fun started for, without the pawl on the winch to halt the cable from running back as the bows rose to the waves we were in a pretty fix. Even the strongest among the crew were powerless and the winch handle inflicted much damage to those of us who tried to control it — a feat beyond any one of us. We suffered two sprained wrists, a broken nose and innumerable bruises and abrasions. Finally, we rigged a stopper and soon had the cable stowed safely below.

Then, under one engine and with its shaft groaning and complaining, we made for Yarmouth. The people ashore had heard the noise of the previous night's action so, as we steamed up the river with the crew fallen in on the foredeck, we were cheered as wounded heroes. The deception was completed by the two who had their arms in slings and the remainder who were covered in sticking plaster. Although our part in the action had not been of great consequence it was pleasant to realize that we were appreciated even though our cheers were obtained under false pretences.

We stayed in Yarmouth for about a week while waiting for a berth at Brooke's Yard in Lowestoft during which time we emptied our petrol tanks and prepared the boat for the slip. Eventually, we were towed out to sea by a small motor boat where we lay, just outside the harbour mouth, waiting for the tug. We were lying with our head to the north when the tug approached from red 45 degrees; I was on the foredeck ready to secure the lines when, to my surprise, the tug kept on coming. Wilkie yelled for me to come aft which I did just as the vessel struck us a shuddering blow on the port bow. At that moment every man aboard 147 rejoiced for the hole in the bow signalled leave, long leave. No more popular man was there on the east coast than that tug skipper.

As previously mentioned, the cox'n and I travelled on leave together and he, after his short visit to my parents' house, went on to Reading.

I had a wonderful few days at home where I met a girl, the ward of an immensely rich man, and became engaged to her when I popped the question on Skindles's lawn; she and I lunched together, dined together and danced each night away together. It was the typical, irresponsible, take-happiness-while-it's-there kind of wartime romance; my leave was all too short.

The day I was to return to my ship coincided with one of the fiercest fire bomb attacks on London resulting in no trains running from Maidenhead to the Smoke. Forlornly, I set off to hitch-hike and, quite unexpectedly, was offered a lift by a motor cyclist; so, riding pillion, I was whisked into the Metropolis, dropped in Trafalgar Square from where I set off to walk to Liverpool Street station.

In and around Cannon Street, the whole city appeared to be burning; it was a sight never to be forgotten. As I strode through the flames and smoke it was not hard to imagine that I was walking through Hell and that the firemen and air raid wardens, silhouetted against the glare, could have been devils (of the nicest type) as they fought with the fires. Every now and then I had to step over burning debris or dodge falling walls and often received warnings for not wearing my tin hat, a piece of apparel in which always I felt ridiculous and uncomfortable.

An exhausted fireman, playing his hose, from which spurted not much more than a trickle of water, called me and said, "Jack do me a favour and hold this hose while I get a cuppa char."

The poor chap looked all in and as I took the hose from him he told me that he had been on duty for many hours and had seen several of his mates either killed or wounded.

I enjoyed playing with the hose but after about an hour without the return of the fireman I decided that I could stay there no longer. The building was, by now, but a smouldering heap of rubble so I put the hose down and continued on my way.

A detour on to London Bridge was irresistible and there, looking back at Cannon Street station, I was reminded of Wordsworth's lines:

Ne'er saw I, never felt, a calm so deep.
The river glideth at his own sweet will;
Dear God! the very houses seem asleep
And all that mighty heart is lying still.

It was strange that despite the fires burning all round the station and the terrible havoc that had been wrought upon my beloved London, there was a sense of serenity on the bridge. The river reflected the flames while around me drifted the acrid smoke but the short span upon which I stood, undamaged as it was, appeared a haven of tranquillity in that wild sea of destruction. It was as though the bridge had been spared to be a vantage point for a declaration of revenge on those Hun Vandals who had perpetrated this crime. To add to the bizarre, macabre scene there was St Paul's Cathedral standing defiant, silhouetted against the glare.

At last I arrived at Liverpool Street station where those wonderfully brave women of the WVS were serving tea and sandwiches as though in a cricket pavilion. The alert was still on but they continued to butter and cut bread, brew tea, chat with us and behave as only English women can in an emergency.

An announcement suggested, that all being well, a train was due in at 04.00 and would leave without delay for Lowestoft. Optimistically those of us going in that direction trooped out on to the platform at about 03.55 and, to our utter amazement the train chuffed, slowly, into the station. With us was a little chap of, perhaps, five feet two inches in height, wearing a bowler hat, a blue serge suit and large, black, well polished, boots; he was an exact replica of Strube, the pre-war cartoon character. Suddenly, the little fellow pitched forward, absolutely stiff, and landed on the line bowler hat first. Another matelot and I had just enough time to jump down on to the track and lift him out of his predicament; he was as drunk as a skunk and when we deposited him, right way up, he raised his hat and thanked us most profusely for, as he put it, 'our gracious act.'

147 was still on the slip when I arrived back at Brooke's Yard; we slept on board but, of course, couldn't cook or use the heads or wash-basins. We ate cold food, wetted the tea ashore and used the yard's lavatories. The other watch was on leave and, all in all, it was a quiet and pleasant time until they returned. I had little to do but indulge my passions for knots, splices and varnishing.

The one nerve-racking chore was duty fire watch; standing, un-armed, on the ML's deck, high above the ground, while bombs dropped in the vicinity was no sinecure and as unpleasant an occupation as any that I experienced during the war.

When the repairs were completed we returned to Yarmouth and the East Coast Convoys. On leaving harbour one evening I noticed a pair of Hotchkiss guns on the bridge of an unmanned and, seemingly, near derelict drifter; Wilkie caught my eye and read my thoughts. The next day we went alongside the drifter and half hitched the two guns which we mounted on the wings of our bridge. However, officialdom? Bumble-dom? call it what you will, intervened and we were obliged to part with our precious weapons. The absurdity of the whole thing was that the drifter just lay alongside and what happened to the guns is anybody's guess. At least we would have given them plenty of exercise.

While on the slip we had been fitted with a contraption, purporting to be a weapon, called a Holman Projector which consisted of a steel tube on a mounting allowing it to be trained and layed. A sight was fitted to the fore end but it was not of much help and sighting, I found, was best done by rock of eye and a silent prayer. This Heath Robinson affair was designed to fire hand-grenades at aircraft with the assistance of compressed air. It was utterly useless although, I believe, a trawler did bring down a plane with it, the only success during the entire war. Besides being useless it was highly dangerous to the user as will be illustrated later. Ours was mounted abaft the three-pounder.

Soon we were ordered to Weymouth and, off the Blackwater estuary I was obliged to undertake a most uncongenial task when, on our port bow, we saw something which turned out to be a body floating in the water.

"Messer, would you mind taking the dinghy and see if you can find some identification?"

"Aye aye, Sir," reluctantly.

"Have you your knife with you?"

"Yes, Sir."

"Be careful when using it that you don't cut yourself, it could be fatal."

"Aye aye, Sir," even more reluctantly.

When I arrived alongside the body I all but returned, at once, to the ML for it was badly decomposed and full of gas. The exposed flesh on the face, hands and neck, was all but eaten away and the remains, stinking to high heaven, were as bloated as a pumped-up pig skin. I knew that should I prick that foul balloon I would not be helping the situation so, gingerly, I unzipped the flying jacket; in one of its pockets I found an oiled-silk envelope containing letters, photographs and the pilot's papers. He was a German.

On returning to the ML I suggested to Wilkie that I sink the body with the Lewis-gun. We couldn't leave him floating in that condition or, indeed, in any condition so to send him to his rest in Davy Jones's locker appeared to be the kindest act. After the grisly deed was done we stood to attention for a few seconds and then Wilkie said a short prayer. How strange is war!

From the photographs we gathered that the German had been a most handsome chap with a pretty blonde wife and two lovely daughters aged about four and six. What a different man he had been from that stinking mass of rotten flesh.

Wilkie insisted on examining my hands for the slightest scratch and watched while I washed them and my knife in some disinfectant which he produced from the First Aid cabinet. I felt like a shower to cleanse myself but had to be content with just the wash. The German's papers were sent to the Red Cross.

From Weymouth we did several patrols off the enemy coast the reason for which Wilkie did not share with the crew. Indeed, the charts were removed from the wheelhouse so we could but guess from our courses that we were somewhere off the western end of north France.

On one of these jaunts off, I suspect, Le Havre we spent three days at sea enabled to do so by a deck cargo of several hundred extra gallons of petrol. Wilkie was on the bridge most of the time so, early on the third morning when we returned to Weymouth, he took the opportunity of a few hours' sleep. Somewhere around dawn, in fog, I was on the bridge with the 1st Lt. when we heard what we thought was a ship ahead steering straight for us as the noise became louder and louder. Something was not right, I was not so sure that it was a ship and, suddenly, the penny dropped, we were approaching the Chesil Bank. Without thinking of protocol I called down the voice pipe, "Hard-a-port, stop port." Up the voice pipe came, "Hard-a-port, stop port, Sir." As we swung round the breakers on the bank were visible. I had given my first order on the bridge of an HM ship and, what is more, it had been obeyed promptly. Wilkie was on deck without delay and the 1st Lt. was decent enough to tell him what had happened. A new course was set for Weymouth.

Just before we sailed on another of these patrols two members of the crew, I forget who they were, brought on board a fat, tame rabbit which they had pinched from a hutch. It was intended that the poor animal should provide our dinner on some future occasion. To this end we drew lots as to who should perform the execution but, as each time the short straw was picked the recipient refused to carry out the dastardly deed, the idea was vetoed. The rabbit seemed to enjoy his hours at sea and was unaffected by the boat's motion. On our return to harbour he was returned to his hutch, during the hours of darkness still, no doubt, to end up as someone's dinner. He was a well brought up rabbit for the mess-deck was almost as clean when he left as it was when he came on board.

On another occasion we took two Royal Marine officers over to France together with their canoe which they paddled ashore. They were brave men.

Later, an Army officer came on board just before we sailed and disappeared into the wardroom. When we were at sea he emerged, dressed as a Frenchman in civilian clothes and joined Wilkie and I on the bridge. Without warning, my CO turned to me and said, "Would you mind pulling this officer ashore when we arrive off the French coast? Oh!" to the pongo, "this is Able Seaman Messer RNVR."

Rather bewildered I replied, "Of course, Sir."

Then I was given a fuller explanation of the exercise to which Wilkie added, "I shall wait X minutes for you and then sail with or without you. At the first sound of gunfire or any other sign that you're spotted I shall be away."

There was a short silence which the Army officer broke. "Are you still game to take me?"

Rather lamely I replied, "Of course."

"Good man," ended the conversation.

The dinghy's oars had to be muffled, this I did with stuff brought on board by the soldier. It was a dark night and, in the tense atmosphere that prevailed, the blackness almost clung to one. No talking was allowed, no lights and, of course, no smoking. We sounded our way in at dead slow speed, the lead being lowered gently over the side to avoid splashes. When we were sufficiently close to the shore the engines were stopped and we glided to a halt; fenders were placed in position and the dinghy lowered into the water. In I got and held the boat against the fenders while the soldier settled into the stern, he had taken off his shoes and socks and had rolled up his trousers. Wilkie handed me a revolver and a small hand compass; at a nod from him I pulled away from the ML and headed for the beach on the course which I had been given to steer.

Every dip of the oars sounded like thunder while, at every second, I expected to see tracer bullets heading towards us. It was so dark as to appear that we were cutting a swathe through the blackness, a swathe that could be seen for miles. I rowed with extreme care to avoid both noise and splashing; when we came to the shallows I turned the dinghy stern first to the shore and let the waves take her in with help from the oars until we grounded. The soldier shook my hand, mouthed, "Thank you," stepped out of the boat which floated without his weight, gave me a push off and disappeared into the night. Now, I was alone a few feet from enemy occupied territory but even then sat on my thwart and admired the courage of a man who could wander off into that enemy territory without any apparent qualms. For myself the thumping of my heart reverberated through the darkness and I could see imaginary Germans everywhere; I felt for the revolver which was tucked into the top of my right sea boot and wondered what use it would be if I was discovered, very little I realized. Being hot blooded I was frightened of myself for I knew that the odds were on me using it if I had the chance and, at the same time, appreciated how foolish I would be to do so.

So, I started back on the reciprocal of my original course; 147 was displaying an intermittent, faint blue light for my benefit. Again every dip of the oars sounded like thunder while, being alone, added to the nervous tension; it is far easier to be brave or simulate braveness, when in company with others. As yet the blue light was not visible, the ML was a small target easily to be missed; I wondered how much time had elapsed since I had left her. I felt cocooned in the darkness, indeed trapped in it. The number of thoughts which can pass through a man's mind in so short a time is truly amazing. I was making mental plans on how to reach England should I miss 147, what course to steer and where

I might land if successful. How near to England would I be at daybreak or, conversely, how close to the French coast? What if I was spotted by a German plane? Would it bother to report me? If spotted by the RAF would they report my position? What were the chances of being picked up by an air rescue craft or warship of either nationality? What if I was taken prisoner, the one thing I feared above all else?

All the time I had been pulling steadily, occasionally glancing over my right shoulder searching for the blue light; it was not visible ahead and a mild panic vibrated through me for I felt that I had been rowing, on the return course, for as long as I had been on the outward one. Taking control of myself I shipped the oars after turning the boat through 180 degrees and sat and scanned the darkness over the stern. Was that the light away to starboard bearing green 135 degrees? I kept my eyes glued to the position and, yes, there it was again. Out with the oars and away I pulled and soon came up with the beautiful shape of the ML. I climbed aboard and the dinghy was being hoisted even as we were sliding, slowly and silently away from France.

Our next port was Dartmouth and there we spent two or three pleasant weeks. We did several patrols in the direction of Ushant the reasons for which I could not establish but we were in close communication, continually, with the radar at Dartmouth. During the day a German reconnaissance plane would circle us, out of range of the guns which it expected us to have but didn't; we would exchange greetings each glad, I am sure, to see the back of the other.

On returning from a beery run ashore with sparks and the cox'n I secured the dinghy to the ladder and went below when sparks in a worried voice said, "Where's the cox'n?"

We looked for him but he was not to be found so we presumed that he must have fallen off the ladder on climbing aboard. How did we not see him? A more likely suggestion was that he leant over the guardrails to be sick and toppled over into the river, this proved to be what had happened. Without delay the cook and I set off to look for him; a strong ebb tide was running and I hadn't much hope that we would find him and, if we did, it was unlikely that he would be alive. I let the dinghy drift down from the ML on the assumption that it would follow the course taken by a drifting body and, thank goodness, luck was with me. He was unconscious but alive; the cook held on to him, keeping his head above water while I pulled back to 147 where willing hands soon had him on his bunk. By then both the cook and I were exhausted but that excellent chap the MM took charge. The cox'n was, by now, blue but the MM

117

emptied the water out of him and then applied artificial respiration; a large tot of neat rum completed the cure. In the morning the patient was as right as rain.

Mountbatten's destroyer flotilla was operating from the port and a damned nuisance he was for his boats would enter and leave 'full ahead and full astern' to the discomfort of every vessel in the anchorage. On one occasion, I was returning to the ML in the dinghy which, laden down with stores, had very little freeboard. In came Mountbatten and the subsequent wash had every boat snatching at its moorings and all but sinking me. I managed to get the little boat head to the waves but not before she had shipped a lot of water. All this took place close to the jetty steps where the harbour-master happened to be standing; after several similar episodes involving others he asked Mountbatten to be more careful and more considerate. Whatever was said must have taken effect for, quite suddenly, the destroyers came and went at a reasonable speed.

Somebody was kind enough to loan me a small sailing boat in which I made several solo trips up the Dart. Lazing in the sun with a book and drifting peacefully with wind and tide was a pleasant variation from life on the lower deck.

Dartmouth possessed the best fish and chip shop that ever I have known. It was crowded out each night but the cox'n had a way with him so we were always sure of something to eat. A few beers, two pennyworth of fish and a pennyworth of chips helped to make a good run ashore.

From Dartmouth we went to Plymouth just in time for one of the heavier raids on the city; it was not enjoyable.

After a couple of days we sailed east towing a cutter for delivery to Dartmouth. We had trouble with the tow which persisted in yawing all over the place so the cox'n suggested that he should get into the boat and steer it. Off Start Point we looked astern and there was no cutter at the end of the tow rope, it was drifting ashore, very smartly, on to the rocks on the east side of the point. We were all guilty of extreme carelessness in neither seeing nor nearing the cox'n's departure for, later, he told us that he had been yelling at the top of his voice.

"Messer would you mind . . . ." I hauled in the towrope and coiled it down in the dinghy's stern and then bent another warp on to it which was secured to the ML. I got into the boat taking a heaving line with me and pulled for the cutter a not too difficult task for there was a strong set with me; as I rowed I payed out the warp astern of me. Wilkie had not wished to approach too close to the cutter and when I came up with it I could see why for rocks were sticking up everywhere. The cox'n soon had the heaving line inboard, I bent it on to the towrope when, at a signal, the ML pulled us both out of danger. From then on a hand was posted in the stern to keep an eye on the tow.

From Dartmouth we returned to Lowestoft in company with the SO of the flotilla, Lt. Harris RN. Before we went to action stations on passing through the Straits of Dover, (a normal procedure), Wilkie had expressed a wish that I man the Holman Projector should we be attacked by aircraft. I demurred at this as I preferred the Lewis-gun but, as is the way, the Skipper's will prevailed.

Off Dover a Nazi plane appeared, I loaded the Holman Projector by drawing the pin from a grenade which I dropped down the tube. The plane circled us, warily, before diving from the landward side with his machine-guns blazing; I waited until I thought that he was in range and fired, the loading-number had another grenade ready which he dropped down the tube. In this fashion I managed not more than three or four shots at the German who, for some strange reason, dropped his bomb well clear on our port quarter. I had noticed, too, that his attack was not directed at the ML but a trifle astern of us. Perhaps he had completely under-estimated our speed or, perhaps, he was not too keen on a close engagement. When he passed over the stern the German was not much above mast height and the pilot was clearly visible. Round he came again on a repetition of his previous run but this time there was no bomb and my damned weapon misfired; this necessitated tipping up the tube, catching the grenade, tossing it over the side — well clear — and then reloading that fiendish invention. All this while the Nazi was sweeping us with his guns and our craft was pitching and tossing in the choppy sea. I swore aloud and fiercely at Wilkie for his indifference to my health although, from the bridge, came equally loud shouts of encouragement. On the German's last attack a few more grenades were tossed at him when the bloody thing again misfired; very nearly did I throw the recovered grenade at the bridge.

After the enemy had gone Wilkie agreed that the Lewis-gun was a much more efficient weapon than that ridiculous Holman Projector; for if it had not jammed, which it was sometimes prone to do, a far more steady and accurate fire could have been maintained.

During the brief battle our cook had poked his head out of the messdeck hatch to see what was happening when, as the pilot was pulling away to port on his last run, he sprayed the ML and a bullet hit the cook's steel helmet a glancing blow knocking him down the ladder and, somehow, on to his stove, seat first. We were a lucky ship and that man was even luckier for his helmet was badly dented but not pierced and his sole wound, besides shock, was a slightly scalded *derrière*. Their Lordships provided him with a new pair of trousers in lieu of those damaged in action.

On arriving at Lowestoft we went to Brooke's Yard where slight damage to the rudder caused by the German's bomb was made good and a Bofors gun was fitted on the foredeck. At last we had a gun that was of some use; if only we'd had it, standing proud on the foredeck, when we had met that E-boat. If only, if only! Here we were, twenty-one months after hostilities had commenced and it had taken all that time to provide us with an effective weapon; at last we were a warship. Those poltroons of politicians who were responsible for our nakedness at the outbreak of the war should have been required to man the antiquated weapons with which they condemned us to combat the highly organized and well armed Germans.

We acquired a new 1st Lt. who came straight from *KA* after a few months of lower deck sea time and who fancied himself as a martinet. Wilkie arranged for him to give me a grounding in navigation prior to my departure for Brighton. This was good news as I was beginning to have doubts about leaving 147. He and I never really hit it off and, on reflection, I must take most of the blame for, rather arrogantly, I felt far more able to do his job than he was and, consequently, was inclined to hinder him more than help.

We were back on the East Coast Convoy run. One morning as I was cleaning up after entering harbour, inadvertently I let off a fire extinguisher in the wheelhouse; foam was everywhere and so were my epithets. Wilkie's reaction was in character and very calm.

"I don't think it fair to ask . . . . (the rating responsible for the wheelhouse) to clean up this mess, do you Messer?"

So I set to on a job which allowed me very little sleep before we sailed that evening.

The base CO at HMS *Mantis*, Captain Stoker RN was a one-eyed ex-actor who had returned to the service for the duration of the war; he was an officer with whom I was on good terms. Being very keen on cricket he had arranged a match between *Mantis* and the Army. My name was on the team sheet despite the fact that we were due to sail at 18.00 that evening for, unknown to me, Stoker had persuaded Wilkie to let me play, promising him a stand-in should it become necessary.

The Army batted first and later I opened for the base and was still there at tea. As I had no knowledge of Stoker's deal with Wilkie I asked

120

him what I should do as 18.00 was fast approaching.

"You stay there, my boy, get as many as you can, beating those Brown Jobs is far more important than the bloody Huns. Besides I have spoken to your CO."

Half reassured I continued after tea but was caught, eventually, in the slips having a go because, believe it or not, I couldn't bear the thought of 147 going to sea without me. My stock rose with Stoker for we won comfortably and I had made some runs.

Although I had a few bangs with the Bofors at enemy aircraft in Lowestoft I fired it, in anger, at sea on only one occasion. We were part of the large escort of what must have been an important convoy which was attacked by enemy aircraft; at last the old boat was able to stand up for herself and nobody was happier than AB Messer to be behind a proper gun giving as much if not better, than we were receiving. Both Wilkie and I thought that we had brought down one of the Nazi planes and on the bridge, after the action, our conversation went something like the following.

"Well done, Messer, we got one of them."

"I thought so, too, Sir."

"There is not much point in claiming it with all these senior officers (destroyer captains) about."

"Why not Sir?" rather aggrieved.

"Their claim will take precedence over ours."

So we didn't claim it. That was in keeping with Wilkie's character for, even if he had been on the gun himself he wouldn't have claimed it. he was far too self-effacing and a man who steered clear of any form of controversy.

There was no sign of my leaving 147 for KA and, soon, the axe was to fall. Wilkie called me to the wardroom and, with a very grave face, explained that the SO of the flotilla would not endorse my departure. The reason given was of a personal nature and had nothing to do with my ability as a sailor or fitness to be an officer. To help ease my obvious disappointment Wilkie added a transparent untruth when he said, "The SO does not like RNVRs, he does not really like me."

When I challenged him with the real truth he could only reply, "I am sorry Messer."

I was flabbergasted, to spend the remainder of the war on the lower deck was unthinkable. Wilkie was as distressed as I was but offered little hope of a change of mind by the SO. Deep in my heart I knew that a second chance was unlikely unless I could get away from 147 and

Lowestoft. The SO had refused to endorse a previous, but different, recommendation of Wilkie's on the same flimsy grounds as those concerning my commission.

I was too discomforted to think clearly so left things as they were for a few days and then had another talk with Wilkie. I put in a request to see Stoker but doubted whether he would overrule the authority of the SO. I asked Wilkie about passing for the hook (becoming a leading seaman) but he reminded me that I would need the SO's endorsement for that.

It was necessary for me to talk the whole thing over with Stoker; I had a good idea what the SO had against me, Wilkie knew and it was vital that Stoker should know for then, perhaps, with the air cleared a proper decision could be made concerning my future.

I had Wilkie's backing in this move but before anything more could be done we sailed for Harwich. There all my instruction ceased although neither Wilkie nor the 1st Lt. put any obstructions in my way when I borrowed charts and instruments in an endeavour to keep up with my navigation. I was utterly confounded and did not know which way to turn. The loneliness of the lower deck manifested itself for, without help from the wardroom, a matelot's lot is pretty hopeless. I cursed Wilkie for his apparent indifference to my lot but, in reality, there was little that he could do other than attempt to strengthen his own recommendation which he did to no avail. Anything more would have prejudiced his own position.

In Harwich, when in harbour, we lay starboard side to alongside an old wooden lightship. Soon after our arrival, when both Wilkie and the cox'n were ashore, we received urgent orders to shift our berth. The 1st Lt. took charge with me on the wheel; he gave me a ridiculous wheel and engine order which I knew would land us in trouble so, as politely and tactfully as I could, I said up the voice pipe, "The Skipper doesn't do it that way, Sir."

"You obey orders, Messer."

"Aye aye, Sir."

We ripped off all our starboard depth charges on the lightship's cathead and the subsequent panic over whether they had been set to safe was something to behold.

At last we arrived at our new berth alongside one of the jetties where Wilkie and the cox'n were waiting for us. When he stepped on board it was the second time that I had heard the Skipper really let go; that damn fool 1st Lt. deserved all he got.

Then my luck changed for very soon after when ashore I ran into Guy Fison who, after our initial greetings, exclaimed, "You still on the lower deck Messer?"

"Indeed Sir."

He asked me the reason so I told him the story, but without my suspicions of why the SO had acted as he had. Within twenty-four hours I was lunching with the base Commander at a local hotel and the next day I had an interview with an elderly Admiral who was most kind and understanding; he asked me very few questions pertaining to the Service but our conversation was far ranging and covered such subjects as sailing, books, the political situation and, oddly, Kipling's verse. It was reminiscent of talks with my housemaster in his room.

The following day I went for a medical when, outside the MO's office I chatted to an AB who told me that he was on the last leg of 'working his ticket'; proudly, he boasted how he had been able to fool the doctors and, indeed, continued to do so for when he came out from his examination he raised his right thumb and said, "I've made it." I was so incensed by the chap's behaviour that I was on the point of telling the doctor but on second thoughts I realized that it was none of my business and that the Navy was better off without him. It was he who had to live with his conscience, if he had one.

I was passed fit and the next day set off for HMS *King Alfred* via HMS *Victory* (Portsmouth barracks).

Wilkie was as happy for me as I was for myself, he was not a man to show his emotions but his handshake was warm and friendly. We had spent nine months together during which time we came to rely on each other in the many adventures which had befallen 147. For a very brief moment I grieved at leaving the ship.

The cox'n's farewell was equally genuine as had been our friendship; he was the best type of RN sailor and there can be no greater compliment than that. Despite our protestations of eternal friendship I never saw him again, for which both were to blame.

The MM gave me his address in Beccles but I did not take advantage of it; the rest of the crew were not sorry to see me go.

I acquired much practical knowledge aboard 147 and left her a far more able seaman than when I had joined her. From Wilkie I learnt shiphandling and from my own experience and, by watching and listening to others, a fair grounding in seamanship and navigation. My two years on the lower deck had given me a deep and realistic understanding of my messmates which was to stand me in good stead when I became an officer and, eventually, had my own command.

I was in Portsmouth for about one week. In the barracks the CW candidates had their own mess and were expected to be smarter than smart but ashore was where the dangers lay for one slip, resulting in being picked up by the patrol, could mean a return to general service. While I was there one or two poor fellows suffered that fate for misdemeanours which, normally, would have been hardly punishable.

Sunday Divisions in Portsmouth was a most pusser event when the entire barracks paraded. On the occasion in question while the Wrens were marching to take up their position, the voice of the Chief GI in charge of the parade rang out:

"Wren No.3 in the front rank, keep the cheeks of your arse together."

The poor girl started to cry, the Wrens' formation broke up in consternation, every man was amazed and the GI was ordered off the parade ground. Apparently he had been full of rum; what happened to him I did not hear but something pretty severe no doubt.

From Portsmouth we went to Mowden House, a peacetime prep. school in Hove where was housed the Admiralty Selection Board; it should be mentioned that having got so far very few if any failed this hurdle. There unexpectedly but delightedly, I remet Paul as well as a signalman, Gordon Davidson, whom I had known in *President*. The latter had been in *Kelvin* in the Med. and, like me, had given up all hope of reaching *KA* until, suddenly one day he was told, quite out of the blue, that his relief had arrived. On transit to England Gordon had met a Hull RNVR rating called Fuller who, also, had given up all hope of a commission; his salvation came when the destroyer in which he was serving, *Kipling*, was sunk off Crete and he found himself on the way to Brighton.

In our division, Drake, there were several other London Division RNVRs whom I had known in peacetime; the remainder were mostly Hostilities Only conscripts or volunteers who had done but a few months at sea. It was a complete travesty of justice that the RNVRs had to wait two years for, as we had gone to sea as ratings, we were considered not to have been automatic officer material, and, in reality, were obliged to go through the same gruelling tests as the RN Upper Yardsmen while the conscripts were selected as future officers at their first interview. Another thing that got my goat was that men up at University when the war commenced were not obliged to do any lower deck sea-time whatsoever and went straight into the service as officers. However it was ever thus.

At Mowden we had another medical; by now one of my eyes was

weaker than the other so I was obliged to read the test with my right eye each time a ruse which, thank goodness, went unnoticed. Then came the Selection Board. In my case the first question was did I sail, an easy one to answer and expand on; then followed a pretty penetrating interrogation on my time at sea and, finally, questions on the rule of the road for both sail and steam. All the officers on the Board appeared to wish us to pass and none were hostile in any way in fact, so helpful were they, that I, for one, gained in confidence as the interview progressed.

On passing the Board we were issued with white cap bands and were officially known as Cadet Ratings. We were billeted in private houses which was complete bliss when compared to a hammock and the messdeck.

From Mowden we went to Lancing College where it was just like being back at school. We slept in dormitories, ate in the refrectory and attended the beautiful chapel each Sunday. Several times a week we played Rugby on the extensive playing-fields. One match was between the UK Cadets and those from Australia and New Zealand which we won handsomely so a challenge was issued for a return under Antipodean Rules which we lost heavily. We began to become alive again at Lancing.

On my first weekend leave I travelled to Camberley to see my fiancée who had joined the ATS, it was to be our first meeting since becoming engaged. I arrived first at the rendezvous and, sad to say, when she came we didn't recognize each other! After a good dinner we decided to call the whole thing off. The sale of the ring considerably assisted my financial situation.

After six weeks we moved on to *King Alfred*, itself, in Brighton where I lost touch with Paul perhaps because the cadets were divided up into classes but precisely why I have forgotten. Gordon Davidson, Fuller and I were a trio; we had no intention of returning to the lower deck and worked like devils, seldom did we go ashore and then only for a couple of beers. Most nights saw us swatting.

The highlights, for me, at KA were my meetings with Beatrice Lillie; her son Robert Peel was a friend who, on a couple of occasions, invited us to dine with his mother who was living at the Grand Hotel. She was as much a character off the stage as on it. Poor Robert dipped and was ushered out of KA at immediate notice without being allowed or able to say goodbye to his friends. He went to DEMS (Defensively Equipped Merchant Ships) as a gunnery rating and, within a few weeks, was killed in action. Poor Beatrice Lillie was heart-broken.

The life at *KA* is well documented in a little book by Mrs Judy Middleton so there is no need for me to duplicate it here. Enough to state that in the three months at *King Alfred* one worked hard and learned a lot. Towards the end of the course one was given the nod that it was safe to order one's uniform.

In Drake Division the first three passed out with record marks and I was third which enabled me to go to MTBs for they, together with destroyers, took the most successful candidates. Both Gordon and Fuller went to destroyers.

Came the day when we crossed the road to the tailor of our choice and donned our uniforms prior to the passing out parade. All I felt was a great relief at being back in a collar and tie and away from the petty restrictions of the lower deck. I had no sense of triumph and, like Gordon and Fuller, no wish to celebrate. It will be remembered that when I was sitting in the bus outside *President*, just over two years previously, I had felt that I was in fancy dress. Herbert Messer inside but Herbert Messer Able Seaman outside; now I felt complete, myself both inside and outside.

My years as an officer are not relevant to this book nor are they of much interest being little different from hundreds of others.

After leave I went to the Coastal Force training establishment at Fort William, HMS *St Christopher*. From there I returned to Chatham for a few days and what a change from earlier sojourns in the barracks. This time being 'shaken' in my own cabin by a pretty Wren steward bearing a cup of tea. The wardroom in the barracks is a particularly handsome one and, again, the contrast between it and the messdecks made one even more aware of one's changed circumstances.

My first operational appointment was to Lowestoft where I became the third officer in MGB 88. Instead of falling in outside the MAA's office I had received a letter from their Lordships directing me. 147 was not there when I arrived but Sparks was, in a different boat; it was difficult for both of us and we decided to ignore each other.

The officers' mess at Lowestoft was the Royal Hotel and, on my last night at the base Wilkie arrived back. Meeting him again on an equal footing was odd for both of us and for some reason we were shy of the other and acted like strangers.

I was appointed to MTB 333 as 1st Lt. to the SO of a flotilla of MTBs to be based on Port of Spain Trinidad. Once again I was lucky with my CO, Lt. H. Barbary RN, with whom I formed a close relationship and from whom I learned a considerable amount. What is more his confidence in me gave me the confidence a fledgeling officer needed.

After nine months in the West Indies we sailed the boats to Long Island Sound where they were paid off. Then came three wonderful weeks in New York to be followed by an appointment to an LCI (Landing Craft Infantry) as the Ocean CO for, by now, I was a Lieutenant.

An adventurous crossing of the Atlantic in the LCI saw me in Gibraltar where I stayed for a short time sleeping in the Cunarder SS *Scythia* which was in dry dock after being torpedoed. It is worth mentioning that ashore I met the Commander of HMS *Nelson* who, on hearing that I had done my RNVR training in the ship, invited me on board for dinner. Again nostalgia came to the fore as I compared the wardroom with the signalman's messdeck.

From Gib. I took passage in HMS *London* to Malta to pick up the Woolworth Carrier, HMS *Tracker*, for my return to the UK.

After a short spell at Weymouth, the MTB training base where I did the CO's course, I was appointed to MTB 286, in command, to be based at Madras as part of the 17th Flotilla. Again I was lucky with the senior officer, for Lt. Hamilton Meikle RN was as nice a chap as one could wish to meet.

After a few months our usefulness at Madras was exhausted so the most senior officers were despatched for home. I was waylaid in Colombo and ended up as 1st Lt. of the Coastal Force depot ship HMS *Kedah* which, in peacetime, ran between Singapore and Penang. She was most comfortable and as the CO never appeared I assumed command of her and was confirmed as her Captain and drove her up to Calcutta as part of the escort of a large convoy.

However, I was obliged to undergo an operation for cancer in Colombo and when recovered was flown home to the UK. After two months of deep X-ray treatment at Mount Vernon Hospital in Northwood, Middlesex, where my parents were then living, I arrived back at Lowestoft in the 22nd Flotilla. The radiologist who was treating me, Professor (now Sir) Brian Windeyer would not at first countenance my return to sea, but when I explained that the crews of MTBs lived ashore and operated rather like bomber pilots he relented. I was given permission only if I gave him my word that I would return to Mount Vernon for check-ups at regular intervals on the days which he stipulated. I gave him my word and kept it.

From Lowestoft I went to Ostend in MTB 187 for the last few weeks of fighting in Europe. VE day saw us at sea, *en route* for Lowestoft, when we received the General Fleet Signal 'Splice the Mainbrace.'

I volunteered for service in the Far East but the medics would not allow that for, regretfully, by now I was declared fit only for shore and home duties in order to keep me within reach of Mount Vernon. That did not suit me so, being 29 years old and having served for the duration I was eligible for early demobilization.

In September 1945 I returned to civilian life but my time in the Navy didn't cease until my leave ended in early December. On the very last day of that leave together with an old friend, Lt. C.R.L. (Dickie) Kemp RNVR, I dined as Hamilton Meikle's guest in the Painted Hall at Greenwich. What a splendid way to leave a Great Service!